Who Moved My Lily Pad

![pond with lily pads and a frog]

Trials and Tribulations of a Brain Tumor

Finding *Your* New Normal

1

Emma

One Two Three Four.
You leave me wanting more.
Into this world you made a showing
And all our tears came flowing.
So tiny, cute, struggling for life;
Your life started with much strife.
But my heart beat to your every breath
And your life now is like Macbeth.
You have overcome all the odds;
We prayed to God and said our lauds.
I love you more each day, month, and year.
I see you grow, laugh, play, and cry your tear.

One Two Three Four.
Five will come and more to explore.
My prayers are answered year to year.
God gave me you and counts my tear.
Emma Brynn you'll always be
The one God chose for me!

This poem is dedicated to my beautiful
granddaughter who makes me very proud, and
keeps me smiling in a way no one else can. She

was born a preemie and had to fight her own battle long before I had to fight mine. She is my pride and joy. She is a reason for me to get out of bed every day. When I found out I had a brain tumor that was initially inoperable, I asked God for one thing: I wanted to see my grandchildren. And he granted me this wish, and she is now a thriving little girl who gives biggest hugs in the world. I now know that I live on borrowed time because God was faithful to answer my prayer. I give God all the glory for my life and for hers.

Acknowledgements

I would like to thank many people who have been beside me every step of the way and have given me the courage to put my words into written form. Writing this book has been both a recovery and a result of my passion to get knowledge out to patients like myself who are treading the waters in the brain tumor world. I have to believe in the possibility that someone will acknowledge our need to have this information and understand that a brain tumor patient wrote this book. Knowing that the language part of my brain has been damaged, it has taken me longer to put these words down than it would a normal non-brain tumor patient. But I am very compassionate to help others so that my experience has a purpose in people's lives. I find that poetry helps me express my feelings in a whole different light and there are poems throughout this book, intertwined between the scariest and most horrifying moments in a person's life.

I want to thank my very talented daughter, who is an underdeveloped artist and has always been able to express herself through sketches and drawings. She is a constant in my life and I have leaned on her

4

more so than I had ever wanted to. I do not want to be her burden in life, but I want to thank her from the bottom of my heart. I also want to thank my dear husband who has seen the changes in me since we were first married, and still stands beside me and holds my hand through every situation. I am so grateful to him for working so hard and continually reminding me that I am still beautiful. My son has been like the root of a big oak tree every step of the way. He has guided me through my struggles every day since my surgery. If it was not for him, I would probably have been cross-eyed and weak. He faithfully visited me every weekend from college and worked with me on every exercise the doctor gave me.

There have been many doctors involved in my recovery process, but there are a few who stand out from the rest. I cannot give out names, but these types of doctors are special, and can be a solid foundation for your own recovery. First of all, my neurosurgeon from UT Southwestern saved my life and believed in me and my strength to fully recover. Secondly, my pain management doctor is my saving grace. As you will read, I am in pain every day of my life and finding this man was just short of a miracle, if it wasn't one. I adore this man's compassion and willingness to help others, and I see him at work each and every month. Without his support and trust in me, I would have given up a long time ago. Kudos to his office staff too. They are the greatest and one in particular, his right hand girl. Last and certainly not the least is my primary care P.A. She jumped on my ship about halfway through this journey and never let go of this heavy anchor I carry around with me today. She understands my every need and knows exactly how to help before I even ask. She has the knowledge and understanding to treat a brain tumor patient that has been through hell and back. Thank you to all of these that support me.

And to the readers of this book I want to touch each and every one someway. I want you to know that this is my journey and it will not correspond exactly with your journey. I hope that these words are helpful and offer healing to those who are searching for answers. I am sure that there will be revisions and rewrites along the way to better express healing that was intended in this book.

Lastly, I am not a doctor, nor am I a health care

professional. I do not wish for this to come across in any way, whether through illustrations or my written words. I only want to write for those who are going through a journey like mine or for those who just need to know that they are not alone. That was my biggest battle to fight: loneliness. Even though I was surrounded by family, the loneliness that comes with brain surgery is unique in its own severity. So I knew that I had it in me to put words on paper to help others, and that is my mission. I apologize if I have left anything out. It is not my intention to hurt anyone or offend anyone by omitting information. I also need you to understand that even though this is a book compiled of my accounts, please take into consideration that my brain is damaged and this will manifest itself in my writing. God Bless everyone who reads this.

The Tumor: The Beginning

It was my 41st birthday and my friends and I decided to have a birthday lunch. I met my friends, and we had a wonderful time enjoying the food and celebrating. As usual, I went home picked up the house, cooked dinner, and went to bed, like any other normal day. I woke up the next morning and noticed that I had a very unusual headache. It seemed particularly strange because it was summer time, and I work for the school district and I didn't really have any stress going on because I was off for the summer. I got out of bed, fixed my husband's lunch, and sent him off to work. I decided I would go back to bed that day and rest for a while to see if my headache would go away. After going back to bed around 8 AM, I awoke at 10 AM and my headache had gotten worse. I decided it was time to take Tylenol and I went back to bed because I didn't feel well. As I lie in bed, I became sick to my stomach because the pain was so intense. I really did not know what was going on. I chalked it up to my hormones and stayed in bed. You may have heard someone say, "This is the worst headache I've ever had in my life," well, this was one of those headaches. At 2 PM I could not stand the pain any longer so I picked up the phone and I called my daughter who worked at the local family clinic. I said to her, "my head is hurting so bad I can't stand it any longer. Could you please come pick me up?" It is very unusual for me to go to the doctor especially for something that I figured was *just a headache*. She came to pick me up and she took me into the back door of the clinic and I went straight to the doctor's room. When the doctor came, he looked at me, and then he gave me a pain shot and a shot for nausea. I had never had a pain shot before today. This information caused the doctor to question what could be wrong with me. He ordered me to go get a CT scan. I didn't argue with him because it's very hard to argue with the doctor who tells you that something major could be wrong such as an aneurysm or a clogged sinus or even a rare brain tumor. So I left the clinic on Tuesday afternoon, and my CT scan was scheduled for Friday.

Friday arrived, and my husband was with me as we entered the hospital and we signed in for the CT scan. When they called my name, it was time for me to go back. I had never been to this hospital for a CT scan, so I did not know what to expect. They

9

laid me on the table and positioned my head to go through the round doughnut-looking machine. The machine did its job and took all of the slices of my head and turned it into a picture for the radiation therapist to look at it. As I lay on the table, I thought to myself, *this sure is taking a very long time*. I noticed that each therapist would leave and come back with a different person, and before long the little window that I could see through had about 10 people looking at my CT scan results on a monitor that faced toward them. I began to get impatient.

"Hello? Could you tell me what's going on and why I've been laying here so long?" Of course what you expected was the answer that I got.

"No, we cannot tell you anything about the scan: you must go back to your doctor and let him explain this to you."

I told them it was Friday and my doctor was not in and I had to wait till next week to go back to see him, and that was what he had told me in person. They informed me that I must go back with the film to another doctor who was waiting on me. Of course, this was a red flag for me. But I did what they said and off I went, worried excessively about what had just happened.

When I arrived at the clinic, I was hurried back to the little doctor's room and my daughter was in there already, waiting for us. My husband and I knew at this point that whatever they had to tell me, it wasn't just a clogged sinus. The doctor began to speak to me.

"You have a brain tumor and it is very large, I am sorry." Then he asked, "Do you know a good neurosurgeon?"

In my mind I felt like I was trapped in a glass jar with an echo in my head saying "brain tooomooor.... And do I know a what?" I was in shock. I had no emotions. I looked up to see that my daughter was crying and my husband's mouth stood wide open. How am I supposed to answer this?

"NO I do not know a neurosurgeon! What the hell? I do not keep one in my back pocket."

"We will try to help you get one." Said the doctor.

"Okay, thank you. Now what? I feel okay, the headache went away and I have not had another one, so are you sure?"

"Yes, and it is a medical emergency," he said.

My life was suddenly put into perspective that day,

11

and the trivial list I had made for my summer became so much less important. I knew I would need to get my life in order. So many people depended on me. How could I possibly take time out of my life for a brain tumor? My son had just graduated high school and I needed to be his mom and get him ready for his new dorm and my dad was not in great health and had his own personal problems too. My daughter was stable however, and had been taking college classes with some help from us, and on top of all of that, my job was going to start back in a month. Well, questions began to fill my mind. *Why this could happen to me? How is this possible?* I went to church, helped others when they needed it, and even gave time to the local nursing home. And this would be a massive blow to everyone around me.

As time passed, I eventually received calls from doctors and I was told that these neurosurgeons had appointments open about 3 weeks out from the date of the call.

"What?" I asked. "I have a brain tumor! How could you put me off for three weeks?" Apparently I was not the only one with a brain tumor in this world; the doctors assured me of this.

So for the next three weeks I began to get my life in order. I didn't have a will, nor did I have a medical power of attorney, both of which I was told I would need. I was only 41. This was not supposed to be an issue until I was well into my 70's. I wrote letters to everyone I loved. I wanted my words to follow them the rest of their life. I wrote down my life insurance policies for my husband and any other pertinent details I could think of. Beyond the logistics of preparing for death, my emotional life was beginning to turn into a downhill spiral. I cried every day and found that I had become a depressed individual. But soon I realized I didn't have the energy to be depressed.

The time came to go to the first neurosurgeon. I took all of the scan results with me and sat in a small, cold room, waiting for them to call my name. As I waited, I took inventory of this place that was allegedly going to help me with this huge problem. I was not impressed and neither was this thing in my head. The doctor said, "My child you are in a bad way." I will never, never forget his words. He went on to tell me that Fort Worth Texas hospitals were not set up to do the difficult surgery that I would need. And now I was even more confused

13

than before. What was I supposed to do now? The doctor went on to tell me that the other appointments that I had for other opinions were just a waist of my time and that I didn't have time on my side.

"So, may I ask what am I supposed to do?"

"I know a doctor in Dallas at UT Southwestern and I believe he will be your saving grace."

"Okay. Do I have to wait another 3 weeks to get in to see him? Because I can't believe I have had to wait for someone to tell me these words. This is my life here."

No one could tell me anything beyond that. Needless to say, frustration was just a small concept compared to how I felt. I left his office with my tail tucked between my legs and my eyes full of tears. My husband and I were in shock, and lost.

The next day, my phone rang and a sweet man on the line introduced himself as an assistant to the doctor who was supposedly going to save my life.

"Mrs. Preskitt, I have an appointment for you tomorrow. Can you make it?"

"Well, of course I can make it."

And from that moment on, I was in the hands of angels. More tests and decisions were made. I was

14

adamant that I would not have brain surgery until my son had enrolled and was starting college. This was taking a chance, but the doctors agreed with close follow up scans and frequent visits. It would be September before I had surgery.

The Surgery

It was a typical September morning, and I was supposed to arrive at the hospital at 5:30 AM. so we decided to get a hotel room the night before instead of driving the 65 miles to the hospital in the middle of the night. I had time to mentally prepare myself for what was going to happen. I wrote letters to each of my kids and one for my husband. I had prepped my husband for all of my life insurance and any other important documents such as a living will, and a medical power of attorney. In my life, I would have never thought that at age 41 I would be worried about dying or possibly entering permanent nursing home care. It was a real eye opener. But the time had come, and my type A personality had let it all go.

At 6 AM the doctor came in holding my chart.
"I've been up all night thinking about your surgery and I believe we should not go in around your right ear. I think the best approach is to make the incision in the back of your head." *What?* And that was the last thing I remembered thinking before my surgery. I had prepared for everything. I had accepted the fact that the surgeons would shave my

head, and I had told everyone the exact plan. How could he change plans on the morning of my surgery? However, it didn't seem to be worth questioning. It was already done.

I awoke later the same day around 6:30 PM. after 12 hours of surgery. The pain that I felt was the most unbearable pain anyone could ever imagine. When I came to, the doctor was standing over me, asking me to open my eyes and see how many fingers he had been holding up and whether I could feel my toes. But for me, the aesthetics was the first order of business. I reached up to my head to feel what I could, and to my surprise, my hair was still in the exact same shape as I went in. They had not shaved my head entirely but instead had used a mustache type trimmer and cut a large horseshoe in the back of my head. My vision was blurry and I felt as though my head was going to explode. I had been located to the ICU and each family member made their way in to see me, and I could not care less. All I could think about was when I could have something to ease the pain. I would get a little morphine but it would not touch the pain.

Let me give you a little word of advice, should you

17

ever find yourself in a hospital. Never schedule your surgery on a Friday. The doctor left my care in the hands of the residents. After all, it was a teaching hospital. The orders were left for me and I was left with instructions that were not going to change until Monday when my neurosurgeon returned. I had made it through without any major defects but I felt like I was the defect at this point. Every little noise magnified my brain. I wanted everyone to shut up and stop making the horrific noises outside my room. I begged for them to quit cleaning right outside my room. Of course they were not cleaning but every noise was magnified times one hundred. My family laughed and assured me that the noise was just normal for the hospital.

I had chosen my sister to help me and my husband through the recovery process. After all, guys think like guys, and I wanted someone like myself to take care of the details. By now, it was 8:30 PM and the deafeningly loud speaker said visiting hours were over and all would have to leave. I couldn't image that after 12 hours of surgery and two hours in recovery that my family would leave me in the hands of complete strangers, but that was how it happened. As I lay there alone, horrible thoughts

18

began to enter my mind. I was terrified that I would have a seizure or bleed out and have to have another surgery. All the negative aspects of the surgery were haunting me. I was awake *all* night and no matter what medicine they gave me I never could sleep. I could hear them whisper above me, trying to be considerate.

"I think she is resting now." They said a few times through the night. "I can hear you," I always replied. But it was finally over and I had survived a surgery that my doctor told me he had never seen one nor performed before. I had a headache from Mars and double vision. But all in all, I had been pretty lucky. The meningioma was named and it looked benign. For the first time since June and the diagnosis, I was ready to slowly move forward to recovery.

Why Do I Care?

My book. My life. Why write? Why read? I have so much *stuff* inside of me. One day I decided I was going to write a book. Fiction or Nonfiction? A little of both I suppose, but mostly true as I saw it in my eyes. How far back can your memory take you? Are your memories accurate? Well now, that just depends. Good and bad and other events affect your memory. Perhaps that means my words will mostly be painful. Don't stop reading now. Words can heal. Words can get you through tough times. Words can encourage.

Have you ever stopped to think about how segmented our lives are? I struggled to find the beginning of my story because of this. But, in my heart I knew that I wanted to help others, and that helped me move forward and work through all of the bumps and difficult memories. Perhaps it's easier to write when you have something to write for. I dedicate this book to all who have gone before me, to those who are diagnosed and the w. & w. {which is our own brain tumor language for wait and watch}. You will learn more about "our language" throughout this book.

I could not bring myself to write any earlier than I have. It takes a long time to process what has happened, and then after a brain tumor, simply processing is a major hurdle. Right after the diagnosis you become a family, with sufferings, a medicine chest, suicidal thoughts, and like I said before, a new language to learn and interpret. This book is for my brain tumor family and for all of our caregivers who stand, stood, and have fought the battle.

I will write my heart
I will write my thoughts
Some will speak their part
But it is not our faults
Life deals us each a deck
But a "brain tumor," what the heck?

September 2013

It's my eleven year crainiversary.
Crain☐i☐ver☐sar☐y
noun

The day we celebrate life, the day we had our brain surgery or craniotomy, the day we found a new way to live and look at the changes in our body.

A new language that no one in your family has ever heard: the brain language. Even some doctors don't understand how to use our language and words. Nonetheless, our brain has re-programmed itself the minute our heads were opened. Our words, our thought process, our spirituality, and our vocabulary, all gone? Or just changed.
Grey Matters, Meningioma, Glio's, seizures, benign, malignant, MRI's MRA's, tumors, and so many more. I will do my best to inform and remember what I have learned.

For the record, I support pink and breast cancer awareness. I've lost a really great friend and grandmother to breast cancer. Pink in October but Grey Matters! When? We all know that October is pink, but when is brain tumor awareness? May is when Grey Matters. Brain Tumor Awareness Month is in May in the U.S.

Oh yes we get a little, I suppose we feel rejected, partially because we do not get the recognition or the…*um*…well there goes my vocabulary. This happens to me quite often. Wait, I remember the word. I could play the word game with my husband, which I do a lot, and bless his heart, he does try when he is with me. But I get so annoyed because the word – it's just gone, somewhere floating around in my brain. I keep waiting for the neuro lightning bolts to connect. Sometimes they do, and wow what a celebration I have. Just me, no one else could ever understand. But, back to the word…um…acknowledgment.

My grandpa had Alzheimer's and I was a caretaker for him. I remember how little by little he lost his words, and his ability to recall people's names and faces. Then came his anger and ability to rationalize. That is what it is like to have brain surgery. I can't think of a better way to describe it. May God rest my Pappaw's soul!

March 2014

My husband woke me up in the morning to drink coffee and I replied, "Emma go back to sleep" and she was not even with us. This is kind of the way it

23

happens. Your mind can't function. It stays a lot in the past, and it hurts to think of the present. You just want all of the bitter memories to go away.

Today is Friday, going to Texas for spring break. Two houses to run, expectations. Can I do this? I have no choice. Where. Why? When will this even go away? If ever? The inside of my mind feels crazy. That's a scary thing to feel.

Where Am I

Where am I?
How did I get here?
I feel a little shy
Like a bird in the sky

Take me back
To the place I knew
Where there is no black
And I feel no blue.

This feeling is real
I am starting to feel
Like I'm in a box
I am in total shock

My life I knew is gone
Now where do I belong?
My family stays with me
But my mind has said let it be.

Springtime

Daffodils, plum trees blooming, Red Bud, and many more living things, each so uniquely beautiful. *How much more wonderful will heaven be?* Every day I look out and wonder how much longer will it be. A minute, hours, days, or years. No one knows the pain I endure each day. Pills by the bottle. The doctors try me on so many different medicines. Sometimes my husband goes with me to the pharmacy because the pharmacist harasses me. I need a name for my brain tumor. Everyone else has a name for theirs, maybe soon. I have a prescription from the doctor but the pharmacy doesn't care. The pharmacist says "well now they have flagged you," a red flag, the FDA {Federal Drug Administration}. This is not because I did something wrong but because the pharmacist puts in my prescription the wrong way. Well like I said, I made my husband go with me. When that happens I can't speak, I can cry a lot, though.

My dear hubby talks for me and he holds me. So many people have to go this alone. I feel for them. I got one bottle instead of four and just went on. It's spring break and I have no choice but to accept it and take more pills than I should for my pain; I hate pain.

Springtime seems like a new day and each new day I hope will be the day that I can think again. I hope that each night as I lie my head down and put the day behind me that when I wake up that *will* be the day that my brain had rejuvenated itself to the old me. Oh, how I want that so badly. Sadly, the same day opens up with the same feeling. It is like that TV show where the man wakes up and starts the day over and over again. My battle cry is to make it through the day and go to bed early just to try again.

I have read articles that give the perfect synopsis of a brain injured person. As I watch the videos, I get angry because instead of the article giving a cure, it gives adaption. I want a cure, plain and simple.

According to the Northern Brain Injury Association,

27

(NBIA) there are triggers where brain injured patient needs therapy. I was not a patient that was given therapy. These triggers are the same triggers I have spoken of in this book. The NBIA goes on to call what happens to a brain injured patient "flooding." They even break it down to two types of "flooding." I have listened to the video several times but ironically they speak way too fast for my brain to pick up on the specific details.

They offer suggestions on how to cope because the brain no longer works properly. The injured brain works more slowly causing the brain to shut down. They are calling this "flooding". It is crucial to avoid flooding because it could take days to recover. Flooding occurs when a patient is in "unintentional mental overload." It is all too familiar to me the signs and effects the surrounding has on me. Triggers such as going to the mall or listening to more than one conversation at a time. Of course, I do try to avoid them but at what cost? My husband gets mad because we missed a game or I just don't want to go out to eat anymore. The NBIA hit all of the concerns of the brain injured patient. It is worth listening to the video on their website at www.nbia.ca.

I will add to this that I watched the video about six times and still couldn't follow along. I tried to take notes but to no avail. The video itself put me into what they call "flooding" but it is just another word for brain overload. I know what my triggers are and how to handle them but on some days I am thrown out there to fend for myself and the strategies they suggest does not work. I wish I could wake up from this nightmare and all would be normal again.

Do you ever look at life inside out? I do! I see people laughing, living, and doing things I can't anymore. Sometimes I am envious to see people laughing, going places where there is loud noise, and crowded places. These spots and events are not options any longer for brain tumor patients. For me, I am home every day like a hermit. I sit and wait on dear hubby to come through my prison door. He works. I'm sitting doing small things that I can do. I have tried so many things. I tried couponing, to tears, it hurts but I can't. I always told my children 'can't' isn't our word. You can do anything and now I am the one saying *I can't*. What else can I try? Let's see, antiquing, no. It's a failure. Selling natural oils, no. Way too complicated for my pain,

29

need to find your "new normal." And it has been eleven years since my surgery. My heart goes out to them because they don't know yet. They need their "new normal". I did not want to write this for this very reason. The new normal is you in another world different than the one you used to live in. You look the same. People see you the same. Even doctors don't understand or see the difference.

They say you're the "lucky one." Basically, you didn't die. But you have extensive problems. You don't sleep, you can't see as well, and you can't speak as you used to, your sensory is going south, and your short term memory is going like dementia. My handwriting is worse. I cannot work, not even an easy job because I might have several good days and then one bad day. That the "new normal" even though we look the same is holding us down like concrete and chains.

There is the family. They treat you like you can cook and clean as always. The holidays... they are hard. I can't even make out a grocery list. And as much as I love my grandchildren, a few hours are enough to put you in bed for days. It takes so much out of you. It's silent. I pray my children will never go through this. Even though my dad had a brain tumor, I wish I could go back and apologize to him for never really understanding the pain and mental anguish he must have suffered.

I want to go through new group therapy but that means more money and we have already spent our life savings on me. More than anything, I wish my children could see the pain.

Our life revolves around so many, many, things now: abilities, driving, pain, and us! For us, brain tumor survivors, every day is a new day when we wake up. We never know what the day will bring. Will it come back? Will I have a seizure today? Will I be able to get out of bed?

How can I just fulfill my responsibility to be a mother, a grandmother, or even sustain friendships? It all turns into isolation. When I had my brain tumor removed I was looked at differently. "Poor," "sad," "that's too bad." Because what we need is support from you! More now than ever. "You're in pain. I don't want to hear it," they might say. I can't blame them; I don't want to hear it either. It's funny how strangers in your life treat you better than your friends and family. Don't me wrong, my children love me. And they would do anything in the world for me. I love them with all I have in me. But they have their lives after all, and at some point they can't drop everything. I want them to be happy and successful and not give me another thought.

My children, well, I hurt them too. After my surgery, I was so lonely. I was married to their dad, who simply told me to get over it and I should be happy. I didn't die. No hugs, no sympathy. I became so lonely I ended up leaving him, packed up everything I had and went to live with my sister. I shattered her family as well. All because I couldn't stand living a lie. Many things happened to my children to make them sad during those times. I'm truly sorry, and wish I could reverse a lot of my actions in order to make them happy. But I was searching for something that would ultimately make me happy. Something that would fill the emptiness and loneliness that no one could understand after having brain surgery. So much had changed. I couldn't fit in anywhere, so I ran away. I looked for other things to make me happy and fill the void inside of me. And I found out real soon that it wasn't going to leave me, that it was going to follow me for the rest of my life. I met a wonderful, loving, supportive man whom I adored and he adored me. And it worked. He listens, holds me, and tells me he understands my pain. He tries so hard and if I cry he is there to pick up the pieces. He tells me he is sorry I am going through this. I hope you have a support system in place. It is crucial to your existence.

Another Day Another Dollar

First of all, brain surgery is not cheap. You will pay and pay and pay. From the time you choose a doctor, you will have a team of doctors ready for every situation in surgery. There are doctors that watch your hearing, speech, sight, and even your limbs. I speak for myself because my tumor was under my brain in the middle of my head behind my eyes. You may need glasses or to see a neuro ophthalmologist. What is a neuro ophthalmologist?

ride home after I was released on Tuesday was bumpier than hell! Some more advice for you is to get you a neck pillow, a memory foam one. It saved my head misery, but the one-hour trip home was awful.

Also, be prepared to see a neuro ophthalmologist for follow-up eye care. I know your neurosurgeon will not automatically send you to one. My eyes were hurting me like stabbing knives and I had double vision. The neurosurgeon wanted me to wait to go see one but I insisted and I am surely glad I pushed for a visit. The ophthalmologist said that my eyes were turning cross-eyed. He said that I needed glasses. I never had any eye problems before. I had to do strenuous eye exercises daily to help my eyes heal from the damage the tumor had caused. He also introduced me to Neurotin. For the double vision, the ophthalmologist prescribed a patch to go over one eye in order to correct it. This was a new concept I had never heard of. I wore this prism on my eye glasses and the patch until the swelling went down in my brain. This took about three and a half months; so don't think you will be great in one month or so. I still wear the glasses today because of permanent damage to the eyes.

Why? None of us really have that answer. Life deals us a crappy hand and we must pick ourselves up and look at these challenges head on {No pun intended}. I am obviously writing to inform you and the rest of the world about the woes of having a brain tumor. You need to be informed as a patient. I remember going into surgery with very little knowledge, and yes it's probably true to not know some of these things, but I can tell you that an informed patient has a better sense of understanding and confidence before the surgery. All of these procedures and processes came as a surprise to me, and believe me when I say that I do not like surprises! I know I have left out a great deal but you will catch some more facts as you read more. I can tell you that your before-life is nothing like your after-surgery-life. You will find yourself surrounded by neurosurgeons, neurologists, primary care doctors, and hopefully a neuropsychologist or two. Certainly, if you have a difficult surgery and a tumor the size of a large plum like mine, Home Health will be at your door for visits. Whew! I went in blind.

Brain Tumor Survivor Support Group

Supporters can relate to any and all things without judgment. Brain tumor warriors are very lonely, however there are several groups, and this is definitely a resource worth using. It is important that you belong to a group, even if you are just being diagnosed or you are the 20-year-survivor. Yes, 20 years, yes! Yes! What do we say or ask in support groups? Oh, so much. Let's start with this post which I can relate to because the story has happened to myself many, many times:

You are faking. Not! This is a monster illness. A silent daily pain maker. How dare anyone say we are faking our pain? And even when I went back to my neurosurgeon he had the gall to say, "well it's not the tumor or anything we did." Well, it's not like we were like this before the treatment/surgery. My words to these people who do not accept or acknowledge a brain tumor as a very bad illness or disease, SHAME ON YOU!

Okay, now that we have that out of the way, let's move on. Here are some more words you never want to hear.

"You do know that a meningioma is benign, right?"
I know you'll read this many times but it is so real and it's the norm when we get to any doctor or clinic. Or even when you go to the clinic, sometimes just ordinary people like your Sunday school class will say this to you. So because it's benign, let me take you where you have never been. Keep in mind I am writing this not only for brain tumor patients, but also for their caregivers, and for ordinary people who just want to know more about how brain tumor patients feel.

"Good morning Mrs. Preskitt, how are you?"
"I am ready today for brain surgery and how are you Dr.?"
Blah blah blah. Drift away to sleep. Doctor starts their plan for you. Did I mention that you have to wait until they study your tumor and then get about seven more doctors and then adjust their schedule to be in the surgery with you in case you stroke out, or you have seizures, lose hearing, have a heart attack, or even die? You get the picture. Anything can go

41

little larger. Because my meningioma was directly in the center of my head, the doctors had to go between the two halves of the brain and down through the middle. With my scalp peeled off and a hole drilled, a tiny little vacuum and other instruments were used to suck out the tumor. I have no idea how to describe in detail. They went into my head. It's a very, very tedious process, in order to avoid damaging the brain. Some people have seizures, some people are awake, and some even lose the use of a limb. This surgery takes time and so much knowledge with the greatest of experience. They must not damage any surrounding tissue in order to keep the patient from incurring further damage.

In the middle of my surgery, the doctor came out and told my husband that they could not get the entirety of the tumor. My husband, thank goodness, said, "Please keep trying, because she will never want to have brain surgery again." So the doctor said he would try his best. Hours passed and he persisted, and was eventually successful. The doctor got all of the tumor out *except* for the origination of the tumor. A brain tumor is an abnormal growth of tissue in the brain. My tumor did have a clearly

Okay, now that we have that out of the way, let's move on. Here are some more words you never want to hear.

"You do know that a meningioma is benign, right?"
I know you'll read this many times but it is so real and it's the norm when we get to any doctor or clinic. Or even when you go to the clinic, sometimes just ordinary people like your Sunday school class will say this to you. So because it's benign, let me take you where you have never been. Keep in mind I am writing this not only for brain tumor patients, but also for their caregivers, and for ordinary people who just want to know more about how brain tumor patients feel.

"Good morning Mrs. Preskitt, how are you?"
"I am ready today for brain surgery and how are you Dr.?"
Blah blah blah. Drift away to sleep. Doctor starts their plan for you. Did I mention that you have to wait until they study your tumor and then get about seven more doctors and then adjust their schedule to be in the surgery with you in case you stroke out, or you have seizures, lose hearing, have a heart attack, or even die? You get the picture. Anything can go

41

wrong when your brain is exposed.

The room is cold, and everything is stainless steel. IV's and 2 ports are in: one in my main vein on the right side of my neck. You can hear your blood swish as it is being pumped into your brain. This is what I remember before the surgery. In surgery, unbeknownst to me, my youngest child went to the snack bar area and saw my neurosurgeon purchasing Skittles candy. My son ran to tell his dad about my doctor and of course, he was in unbelief, because they had been waiting all day. My husband went to see for himself and sure enough there was my doctor. He said he was "taking a break." Who knew your doctor would be taking a break for Skittles during your brain surgery?

I had always thought they would shave my head, so before the surgery, I went and got a nice very short haircut. Before that, I had beautiful, long, wavy hair. Nonetheless, they started by trimming a huge horseshoe shape with a mustache trimmer in the back of my head. Now I will describe something, so if you are squeamish or faint at heart you might want to skip this part, but this is real and will always be a part of my experience and others who

42

have had brain surgery. Understand everyone is different and not everyone will get the same treatment. For example, some will have an ear-to-ear cut and their head shaved, while others may just have a straight cut directly to the tumor's site. My cut, however, was the upside down horseshoe cut. Once the cut is done, blood, blood, blood, going everywhere and then they peel your scalp away from your skull, like peeling your face off completely down to your eyes. Can you just imagine having all of your hair and skin gone? But then there's the skull. Your tumor. My tumor was way past that. Out come the saws, but before that, they put a metal halo on your head/skull and screw it in. I can still feel this screw holes, and it is still tender on my temples where the halo was screwed in. They have to do this to keep your skull intact when they saw your skull like a jigsaw. For mine, the positioning of the hole had been studied for three months, my hole in the head was to be in the right top part of my skull.

Please remember that this is my specific experience and everyone is different, but I continue to talk and write so that this might help someone else one day. The hole was about the size of a half dollar maybe a little larger. Because my meningioma was directly in the center of my head, the doctors had to go between the two halves of the brain and down through the middle. With my scalp peeled off and a hole drilled, a tiny little vacuum and other instruments were used to suck out the tumor. I have no idea how to describe in detail. They went into my head. It's a very, very tedious process, in order to avoid damaging the brain. Some people have seizures, some people are awake, and some even lose the use of a limb. This surgery takes time and so much knowledge with the greatest of experience. They must not damage any surrounding tissue in order to keep the patient from incurring further damage.

In the middle of my surgery, the doctor came out and told my husband that they could not get the entirety of the tumor. My husband, thank goodness, said, "Please keep trying, because she will never want to have brain surgery again." So the doctor said he would try his best. Hours passed and he persisted, and was eventually successful. The doctor got all of the tumor out *except* for the origination of the tumor. A brain tumor is an abnormal growth of tissue in the brain. My tumor did have a clearly

defined border and had no vein feeding it. That is all good. All of that sucker came out. But I was told later, much later actually, that he could not scrape the origination because he was afraid of causing permanent brain damage; I now live with a chance of regrowth at any day, month, or year. In the beginning, I had weekly checkups. I had three-month MRI's, then worked my way up to six-month MRI's, then yearly. And now after all of these checkups, I go back every two years to make sure that damn thing in my head is still not growing.
This brings on a lot of emotions, lots of deep thinking, lots of loneliness, and sometimes desperation if the head hurts worse on some days. Your first thought is: could it be the brain tumor?

And now you have to psych yourself in order to repress the thought of the tumor. This tumor stole my joy, and it stole my life. I do live daily, but nothing is the same. I suppose it never will be. I have titanium screws and a plastic bone flap covering the whole. And a scar of a horseshoe that has what I call dungeons-in-digs in my head. They're like huge boulders and they are so tender to touch. And this was eleven years ago. So many suffer in other ways I can't explain, but I read every

45

Companion Diggity Dog

Today a blessing came into my life
I struggled and toiled but it was right.
You are such a small furry thing
I promise to keep you under my wing.
Teething, chewing, pooping, peeing too
Sometimes when you do I hit you with my shoe.
But I'm here to teach you and love you
To protect you and guard from when I'm blue.
My companion you will always be
I will hold you, thank you, you will see
My love for you will grow like a tree
From the fig to the tree still with needs
Someday we will reverse the roles to play
The end that day and I hope you will stay
On my lap still wanting to play.
That the dulled eyes and wiggly little tails
Just like little boys with pails and snails
But for now little and small
We will wait for you to grow tall.
Diggity dog still jumps at frogs.

The Storm Is Coming

I know this may sound cliché but many, many times, I heard my grandparents say that their bodies hurt at least one part of them. Of course, they would always say a front or a storm is coming and that their bodies could tell. As a little girl, I honestly thought that they were just a little crazy. But now, my head can feel the barometric pressure changing and it always feels like it's going to implode before the storm comes through. And if the rain comes, or a cold front starts to blow through, anyone with meningioma brain tumor can tell you. The pain presents itself like a migraine, but it's not one. It is sort of like arthritis, but really there is no accurate explanation. We medicate by any means available. Then we look for devices. Something like heating pads, ICE PACKS, stimulators, and the list could go on and on. I suppose I might be luckier than most because my pain management doctor is a very compassionate man, and he gives me the means to have strong medicine, but it is still limited. So you have to pick and choose which days are worse, and hope that within the four to five-week time period

Companion Diggity Dog

Today a blessing came into my life
I struggled and toiled but it was right.
You are such a small furry thing
I promise to keep you under my wing.
Teething, chewing, pooping, peeing too
Sometimes when you do I hit you with my shoe.
But I'm here to teach you and love you
To protect you and guard from when I'm blue.
My companion you will always be
I will hold you, thank you, you will see
My love for you will grow like a tree
From the fig to the tree still with needs
Someday we will reverse the roles to play
The end that day and I hope you will stay
On my lap still wanting to play.
That the dulled eyes and wiggly little tails
Just like little boys with pails and snails
But for now little and small
We will wait for you to grow tall.
Diggity dog still jumps at frogs.

47

The Storm Is Coming

I know this may sound cliché but many, many times, I heard my grandparents say that their bodies hurt at least one part of them. Of course, they would always say a front or a storm is coming and that their bodies could tell. As a little girl, I honestly thought that they were just a little crazy. But now, my head can feel the barometric pressure changing and it always feels like it's going to implode before the storm comes through. And if the rain comes, or a cold front starts to blow through, anyone with meningioma brain tumor can tell you. The pain presents itself like a migraine, but it's not one. It is sort of like arthritis, but really there is no accurate explanation. We medicate by any means available. Then we look for devices. Something like heating pads, ICE PACKS, stimulators, and the list could go on and on. I suppose I might be luckier than most because my pain management doctor is a very compassionate man, and he gives me the means to have strong medicine, but it is still limited. So you have to pick and choose which days are worse, and hope that within the four to five-week time period

48

of refills joined with limitations of the pharmacy and the FDA. They do not distinguish the true sufferers from the drug addicts. Just so happens that as I write, In April there have been two fronts in the last week, and I have had so much pain that I have had to use the backup medicine. I'll only get two per week, not refills, but two pills per week. Every doctor makes each patient use the same pain scale: 1– 10. I hate that scale, as I know each and every patient hated it too at some point. When I had the craniotomy, I felt so much pain that any single digit number would be way too small, so I just told them 10-20-30-40. Then I asked them, "Do you get it?" It's been eleven years and I still get anxiety just remembering those days.

I have tried to use my medicine in small amounts because I have learned that the medicine has to filter through all of my vital organs and I have to choose to be a good patient and go by the rules. I do not currently reside in a state where cannabis oil is legal but I have heard that those who are in the legal states sometimes experience massive pain relief and that it can even heal the damaged nerves. I have heard that the FDA has drafted a patent on the oil to establish their role in case the states legalize the oil for medicinal use. With me living in two states because of my husband's job, neither state has legalized it at this point. I am not pro marijuana, but I have done considerable research, and the oil is supposed to actually work. There is so much information and trial studies that proves it can shrink the tumor, put cancer in remission, and/or even kill the pain. So why? I add my name to every list that I can find to help keep the process moving along but the ignorance of the unknown still prevails. I am a Christian woman, and I know that if I never had a brain tumor I probably wouldn't understand, nor would I even try to look into it. It's that old adage that, until you walk a mile in my shoes, you will never know or understand that brain tumor patients are desperate for a cure. And not just to care for brain tumors, but the aftermath also. Please remember, there are so many pediatric brain tumors too. They are manifesting themselves more and more and younger patients and most of them are malignant. When you see them on TV, look deep into their eyes, for they cannot express themselves in the way adults do. I can only imagine how much they are suffering.

Go Away Pain

Rain rain go away
Pain pain is here to stay
My head is going to explode
Their barometric pressure is in the mode
No Medicine nor device can work
This praying – the pressure I just can't shirk
I wish you knew how I feel
Then maybe sometimes it brings me a meal
The days are long, nights are longer
I go alone through the day in somber.
I love you all it makes me cry
Sometimes I wish more you would try.
Pain pain go away
Seems like rain is here to stay.

Stupid Tumor

My house used to be full of laughter
But tumor has changed the after
Two beautiful, a boy and a girl
Feel my heart was such a thrill.
One more to the family tree.
It is a beautiful girl I love to see.
In a moment all did change
Sometimes I wonder if I'm insane
The tumor set me aside
For a year I took a ride
Into a world I never knew
My heart my soul grew very blue.
I hurt the ones I loved
I know that God looks from above.
I blame it on the meningioma tumor
Divorce entered as well as rumors.
But if this happens to you some time
Which part of you do you think would shine?
My love for all never changed
I only had the tumor to be blamed
Stupid tumor, long lasting pain.
I can never do it again!

The Voices

There are so many different stages of life with a brain tumor, and each one is different. As I write about my own experience, I also listen and read about others' experiences. I will never reveal who you are or were, but I will do my best to give you information on different scenarios. I do believe it is important because we are all searching for answers and we definitely do not understand the prepositions "who," "what," "where," and "when." I apologize for saying this, but the doctors do a terrible job on giving you the specifics. They have book knowledge. But there is no way for any doctor to understand our feelings, and the new person inside of us that emerges after surgery, or even moments after the diagnosis. It is sink or swim for the person that has the brain tumor. Shame on the medical field for not providing us with more information and support. At the very least, a hot line or group to attend after surgery should be available. I personally think that a neuropsychologist should be a mandatory supplement to treatment. I know that mine helped me cope in a world I didn't recognize

53

anymore. I was like a new born baby again at age 41.

In order to honor all of those wonderful parents that have lost a child, I will do my best to include a little insight. You have suffered so much. I know your hearts must be aching, hurting, broken, and numb. I can't imagine losing my child to a brain tumor and the role of a caretaker added to parenthood is so burdensome. "I wish more people could understand," is what I hear from so many. The pain and suffering actually goes far beyond the parents. It affects the grandparents, friends, cousins, and everyone involved in the caretaking. I know your pain continues beyond the loss. So, many people, as I have said before, don't know what to say to you. Your life is and never will be the same.

There are levels of grieving, and they are not always the same from one parent to another. We all have painful anniversaries, whether it is a crainiversary or the birthday of a lost child. Do not rush, or say you need to get back to normal. You have to go through so many levels of grieving that no one has a right to tell you when or what normal is. For those of you who watch sufferers, please just provide them support. Take them food, mow their yard, bring toiletries, or give them gift cards to use when they do have a chance to go out and feel better for a few hours. As I write, I do realize I have not lost a child to a brain tumor, but we have all seen the faces of those babies who are suffering and have suffered before. It is real pain.

Who Moved My Lily Pad?

Brain tumors have no boundaries. Husbands, wives, sons, daughters, and more. Every type of human can get them. We don't even know what causes them. There are no proven connections between genetics or environmental factors, even though there have been so many trials and studies. One man stated, "I just had headaches and the test was to prove migraines. My results were just completely and utterly shocking, and I still haven't got over it."

I will try to give other perspectives as well as my own, as every brain tumor has a different story. This particular paragraph will give a glimpse of

55

what brain injury survivors want you to know. This could be the voice of us all. Please just listen and try to understand.

We need a lot more rest than we used to. We all get fatigued. Brain fatigue. For myself, it is hard to put words together that make sense sometimes. Sometimes I feel like push mowing the yard, and I look like I am strong enough. That is probably what you see too. But it hurts so badly the next day, and I stay in bed all day. My ability has become limited, and so have my neurotransmitters. Oddly enough, I must change the way I think. A "new normal." I can finally accept the change, but what about my family? They only know the old me, and they have expectations of the old mom and wife. I have changed. Social anxiety. I used to conquer the world, or so I thought. But now when I walk into Wal-Mart, my brain goes overloads. I cannot function. I know I need a list but my list of items 1, 2, 3, 4, is cut short by item 2. The list doesn't even make sense. I can't even follow a recipe any more. I will get all the ingredients together, and what used to be so easy for me does not come natural for me any longer. I will frequently leave out an ingredient, and the recipe is a flop. I also experience sensory overloads now. If everyone in the room is talking, my brain can't handle all of the conversations. There is way too much background noise for my brain to process. I am not being rude, nor am I being difficult. I have simply changed. I may need more time to talk, process, and find the right word to say. Also, I have been told I tend to become irritated more easily. I may seem to get irritated and it might come across as an attitude problem, but I am trying to tell you that there is a greater problem. Probably a coping problem. Please don't forget, I am in constant pain in my head and I can frequently become pushed beyond my means of coping. And remember, multi-tasking is impossible for me now. I used to work as an administrative assistant at a school where there were many problems coming to me at once. And now I can't, so I don't. This makes me sad. How do you treat me? I am not an ignorant person. I test above average with difficulties. My brain has suffered an injury, but it doesn't make me childlike, or below you in any way. I used to be a very spontaneous person, and yet at the same time, I operated with OCD. My children and husband would say that I am too hard on myself. But now, my constant need to clean is gone. It just is. Please help us with our schedule. My brain

57

needs help with coping and retraining now. At times I may forget where to go, or I may check that I have locked the door of my house three times. My short term memory is gone. After eleven years, it is only getting worse. Telling me that I need to stop will not help. We need your support. Please do not throw negative remarks or be critical to me. It will hurt me, and the box will go up and you will never have an opportunity to help me again. We will also need help with our medicine and doctor appointments. The brain is a remarkable organ. We may or may not get better. After eleven years, I am not only getting older, but it seems that my brain is getting worse. I need love and hope because what is easy for you is extremely hard for me. Our hope is found in our family mostly.

I'd like to point out to caregivers the symptoms of a Traumatic Brain Injury. It can affect a person physically and psychologically. Physical to us, the brain tumor family, means that we are tired and must rest. Physical fatigue doesn't always match our mind to our bodies. I do know from my standpoint, that if I am physically fatigued I will shut down. My emotions take over and my family just stares at me, some even roll their eyes. They don't understand the complexity of my injury.

Questions?

Oh how many questions I have been asked about my experience and how I have managed. For others too, the questions never end. There are so many more answers since I had my brain tumor, but answering specific questions can be tricky because every situation is unique. Even though you may have the same tumor, or grade of tumor, your doctors will have their own ways to treat, and beyond that, there are so many variables inside your brain. I do believe that every decision is an educated guess from a person just like me. I know they have the credentials on a piece of paper and they have spent hours and hours studying, and even practicing. But the honest truth is that, until you get into someone's head and brain, there's no way to prepare properly for the surgery or for the treatment plan. But most definitely, get a second opinion and even a third opinion. And then there is that remote chance that you are in no condition to make this decision of a lifetime. I tried myself! When I finally found someone to say they could help me, I listened, then I said, "okay let's get this thing out of my head!" For me, the brain tumor was always labeled the "thing." Lots of people name their tumors but to me, it was just a thing.

Getting back to the question/answers, I'll try to give you some insight on the mind of the people around me who have asked me questions.

<u>Do I have a Brain Tumor?</u>

What are some of the symptoms of a brain tumor? Early symptoms may begin as a really bad headache, dizziness, nausea, or vomiting. Other symptoms as the tumor progresses could be persistent low grade headache, lightheadedness, which I had, poor concentration, Intolerance to light or vision problems, tinnitus, and more than usual anxiety.

<u>Did I have to have the tumor removed or could I have waited?</u>

Well, I never entertained the idea of leaving a foreign thing in my body. Some people are given the opportunity to wait and watch, or W and W. There are always risks no matter what decision you make. MRI's become a regular routine part of your life.

How long were you off work?

This is a loaded question. My plan was to get surgery in September, stay off work six weeks, and go back as soon as possible. The doctors told me to expect to be off work for six months. I couldn't imagine being off work that long, nor did I know whether my job would be there for me by the time I would be ready to return. What I do know is that when I woke up after surgery, work was the last thing on my mind. I did all I was supposed to do to get well. Wellness was a whole different level than any of my previous surgeries I have experienced. I had physical therapy, occupational therapy, and home health care. September 19 was my surgery day and by then, someone was already claiming my job. So, I worked out an arrangement to work half days starting in December. This was a huge mistake! But I would go against the doctors' orders just to make my presence known and that I was going to beat this thing! The moral of this situation: Plan on being off work at the very least three months and up to six months for the swelling to go down and neurotransmitters to reset. I had horrible headaches and I was exhausted. Bad decision.

Do you do okay in the MRI machine and do they give you sedation?

Yes, follow up MRI's are a must. Do not miss your appointments. They will show any possibility of regrowth and can show you scar tissue which could be causing you all kinds of twitches, unexplained muscle movements, or even abnormal brain activity like seizures, small or big. And as far as sedation for claustrophobia, no they do not give it to you automatically. This is up to you to speak up! Tell everyone, but start with the doctor. Ask for a prescription for anxiety meds or possible IV sedation for the extreme claustrophobia from encapsulation MRI machines. And remember every machine is different. Some machines have mirrors above your head to reflect a beautiful scene or the projection of the outside commotion. These are helpful to the ones that have phobias. Other machines offer music of your choice. Then still, there are what I call "old ones" that just harness your head, throw earplugs in and say this will take about 45 minutes. You have to learn to close your

63

eyes and do deep breathing techniques. Most important of all, ASK, ASK, ASK. Also, remember to ask for a copy of the report mailed to you and a copy of the disc. They usually will give you a copy of the disk while you wait. I keep all of mine just for records or for future reference. It is very important that you do not assume the right people will get your results, and many doctors will want a copy. Personally, I am a veteran of MRI's. Even being a veteran doesn't mean the technician will be nice to you.

Is this memory thing normal, and how do you handle it?

I have short term memory loss and word recall loss. I do the "game" just like most of the meningioma-benign tumor patients. My husband, with whom I depend on a lot, plays it with me. I will say something like, "Can we go to…you know…that place…it's by the river across from the place that has singing?" Then he starts playing the guessing game. Bless his heart. He is not that great, but he tries. I just say, "Oh well, never mind," and sometimes in an hour or a day it will pop into my messed up brain, Just like an "aha!" moment.

And what is VERY IRRITATING is when people, even your own doctors say, "Now how old are you?" I believe it's just your age. NOT! I was fine before and not fine afterwards. I just want to choke them but I guess the darts I throw with my eyes work. It is worse when I am tired or stay out too late, especially when I am sleep deprived, which actually happens more often than you might think. Sometimes my sentences are jumbled and do not make sense, or I sometimes I say something off the wall. My kids just laugh and go on. It is frustrating, but it is normal for brain tumors patients. What I don't understand, is that this happens to so many of us but the neurosurgeons will never accept any blame. I chalk it up to avoiding mal-practice. I have had many tests. I highly suggest a getting a neuropsychologist to give you some peace of mind and it will also show your weaknesses and your strengths. Most importantly, after testing, follow up and ask for advice on how to adjust to your new normal. And I would even suggest taking family members so they can hear this from a professional. Some will think you are faking. It's very frustrating. It has nothing to do with age! Listen up people, we need your support. We need validation.

Do your emotions change, and do you get anxiety or paranoia?

With my brain tumor surgery having been eleven years ago, I often reflect on many things I did. I kept telling everyone I was okay and that I had not changed. They would raise their eyebrows, implying that they had seen a change in me. I was the only one who couldn't see the change. This caused me to feel an immense sense of loneliness. The whole world was turning around me and I was sitting still. The first year, the feeling of loneliness is what I remember the most, and then when someone would whether I was okay, I would reply that I was absolutely fine. I know now that I was very irritable, but with cause. My whole life had been changed in a moment. Then came the anxiety, anger, and panic attacks. I was afraid to be left alone. What ifs drew lines through my mind like air traffic control maps. But I was only 41 years old, and I couldn't make the world stop for me. No one else at the time had had a brain tumor or craniotomy. The more anxiety I got, the more depression set in. You have to get outside of those thoughts. *What if it comes back? Or when it comes back will it be malignant? What if I have a seizure at home by myself?* It became a what if game in my head. Even five years down the road, whenever I ventured into new territory, I got a huge lump in my throat and regressed into panic attacks and depression. When I told the doctor, my family doctor, out came the script book for Xanax and Lunesta for depression. It seemed my pill intake just doubled every time I went. As I stated before, my short term memory didn't help in this area. I had to go get a pill reminder box. I felt like my 80-year-old grandmother except I had much more medicine than she ever did.

Even with the tumor removed, the anxiety stays with you. Anxiety and stress goes hand in hand. I know we all have stress, but if your head is opened up, then you will know what stress really is. I have PTSD. No one really every realizes that you don't have to go fight a battle to have this disorder. We go into survival mode and eleven years later; I am still

67

here. It never ends.

What causes a meningioma brain tumor?

I read that most meningioma tumors are usually benign and could be either from a rare inherited gene or a possible exposure to large doses of radiation such as dental x-rays. And of course, the jury is still out on cell phone waves. For myself, I have recently been diagnosed with Neurofibromatosis. Some say that you can get them from power lines, those big ones that go through pastures that radiate waves that expose us to ions. To this day, I have not read any positive study that shows any of these are true except for the inherited gene. Ironically, my dad had a brain stem tumor and at the time, I was in the eighth grade. I didn't ask questions, but I was scared to death. I know that a lot of time has passed since then, and even in my eleven year run, there have been new techniques to treat meningiomas. Most meningiomas are benign and grow on the meninges, the lining of the brain. When it comes to discovering them, the smaller they are, the better the end result.

Sometimes during surgery, they can get it all out, but there are times that they must leave a small portion of the tumor in order to keep from damaging the brain. I was told that with mine, they had taken it all but hadn't been able to scrape the origin, so I have to have two year MRI follow ups. And I was also told that if it does grow back, the chances of it being malignant is higher.

When can I wash my hair?

Washing your hair is a question for your doctor. Some patients will have staples, while some may have stitches. Likewise, some will have their heads shaved and others, just a small patch gone. I was able to wash my hair within the week after my brain surgery. I did have staples, but one of the aides came in to my room after my surgery and took out my staples only three days after my surgery. The doctor had just told me that I would need to come back in two weeks to get the staples out when, to his surprise, I informed him that they were already gone. I'll admit it was a humorous misunderstanding, except for the fact that I was terrified of sneezing for the next two weeks. My doctor gave my instructions to use a cotton ball with peroxide to clean the incision and just use water for the first couple of weeks. I used a very mild shampoo like baby shampoo until I was comfortable with the healing of the incision. I didn't dye my hair for three months, ladies. I know this is always on your mind too.

Can I ride roller coasters after my brain surgery?

I can tell you from my experience, that I definitely would *not* ride roller coasters after brain surgery. I rode the two biggest ones at Six Flags in Arlington and I felt like my brain was scrambled, and to this day I think it might have caused some damage in my head. I would not recommend that you try the bigger ones that toss you side to side and upside down. Otherwise, have fun and be careful. I did ask my doctor, and he said it would be fine but we all know that doctors, for the most part, have not had their brain cut open and violated.

I am having brain surgery soon. What do I need to pack?

When you go in for brain surgery, there are many

items to consider bringing. However, you should only pack what you need for the hospital stay and have some other items for when you are at home. You should pack your own pillow, an ice pack (don't assume the hospital will have one), something to put on your lips, a U-shaped memory foam pillow. Other items could be your own pajamas, because you will walk down the hallway for therapy. You'll want to bring house shoes, and some people say you will need an extra-long phone charger, but I didn't feel like talking on the phone anyway. I don't think you really need anything more than what you might bring during a regular hospital stay. I would take some paper and a pen and write down things as you think, because after surgery you will not be able to think correctly. Just count on it. My biggest concern was that it hurt to lay my head on the pillow, so concentrate on a good triangle support for your back and the neck pillow. You will need them both when you get home. And hopefully someone will be bringing meals in for you and helping you around the house for a while.

All of these questions and answers may apply to you. I know there are many, many more to add, but these are the common thoughts and concerns for

71

most patients. I think the most traumatic problem for me was my family. Once you look fine, everything will go back to normal for them. For us, we must reinvent ourselves, and attempt to achieve "the new normal."

There Is a Medical Term for This?

Aphasia. Yes, there is a medical term for what you have been experiencing. Kind of a fancy word, so the doctors do not tell us the *real* reason for the madness going on in our heads. You know "that battle cry" the one we can't explain any longer, because our minds, or I should say brains, are scrambling for every word that we try to think of, or even say. Let's say that again, *Aphasia*. I have it. Do you?

According to the Mayo Clinic, Aphasia is a result of another condition, such as a stroke or a brain tumor. There are different types such as Nonfluent Aphasia, which is damage to the language left frontal area of the brain. This sometimes makes words harder to get out and the sentences choppy.

Then there is fluent aphasia, which means damage to the language in the middle, left side of the brain. People who suffer from this can write complex sentences but they don't really make sense because of the misuse of the words.

Then yet another aphasia: Global. This is extensive damage to all the brain language area. People who have this have an all-around problem with use and understanding.

Of course, when I read about all of this, I tend to self-diagnose myself as a sufferer of one type of aphasia. But then I keep reading about another type of aphasia and decide that I might have that one instead. This causes some frustrating internal dialogue. *What the hell? Could we all have both?* Maybe this is why aphasia is not vastly understood in the brain tumor world.

The scary thing about aphasia is that it never gets better. In fact, it is a precursor to dementia. Yikes! It will progress and gradually disintegrate the brain

73

cells located in the language area. There are some who just have small bouts of aphasia, for example, during a migraine. However, it is a very serious, degenerative disease. It can affect your day-to-day activities and overall function. It can lead to severe depression and relationship issues. There are tests that can show your ability; these tests are usually given by a neuropsychologist. Search for a good one: one that has compassion and has experience with people with brain injuries such as a brain tumor or strokes. The neuropsychologist will give you a test to show your area of weakness. But be prepared. Even though the tests are easy, they last all day. Then you will follow up with her and she will help you get through your daily activities with suggestions and exercises to help you keep your language marbles. I've got mine, but they are all scrambled. And yes, I loved my neuropsychologist. I need to see her weekly for the rest of my life but that probably will not happen. I guess that is why I want to tell others to get a good one.

Advancements

It has been eleven years since my surgery. I try to

read and study all the new advancements that have been introduced since then. A lot has happened in the last decade. While I am certainly not anywhere near an expert, I felt like I need to spread the knowledge I have acquired. Recently, according to The American Cancer Society, there are several vaccines that are being used as a trial to influence the tumor by treating it rather than preventing them. The trials are mainly being used on Glioblastomas. However, from what I have read the studies are not funded enough to make a difference. More funding is needed to reach more types of tumors.

Genetics

My pain management doctor told me that studies are being conducted in the field of genetics and how genes affect health. Soon, if not already, a person's genes will be able to tell all. They will reveal what medicine to use, and how it will respond in one's body. This will help in the use of chemotherapy. According to The Sydney Morning Herald, doctors say that patients with brain tumors can be treated with new technology that spares the memory. Currently, they radiate the whole brain. We all know that this causes memory loss and cognitive

75

issues. The new stereo active eradication can be used to precisely apply radiation directly to the tumor.

Radiation- Stereo active eradication: I feel a little freer to give advice in this area because as I write, I am on day two of a thirty-day rotation of radiation. The therapists and doctors are able to precisely radiate the tumor only, which saves the surrounding tissue and close organs. The machine uses a three-dimensional proton beam. It takes minimal time and they have tattooed marks on my body where to set the beam. This makes it relatively easy each time I lie on the scan table. There is also a CT scan inside the equipment that allows for a more accurate guide to the tumor.

As I write these words, more and more research is being conducted, and trial studies are being completed. Dr. Andrew Rochford and Nicholas McCallum write in a column that there have been "few improvements in treatment for brain cancer over the past 30 years," and that "patients are now going to have access to new drugs and management." Another neurosurgeon, Dr. Charlie Teo, states, "The new method completely changes the scene for brain cancer sufferers." We all know that brain cancer does not get the time and research that other cancers get. As part of the brain tumor community, we all push May as brain tumor awareness month, since we all know that October is the pink month. We do not want to take away from breast cancer awareness, but we definitely want the same support as breast cancer. Michelle Heaney from the Cure Brain Cancer Foundation states, "It was unacceptable there had been so little progress on brain cancer treatment over the past three decades." She goes on to say, "When you are a patient and when you're a sufferer, the only thing you do have is hope." As a 12-year survivor, I agree that we fundamentally rely on *hope*. We cling to hope because that is all we have. The brain tumor community is a close knit family. We know that there are books out there written by doctors, and the information is great, but not one of those authors have had a brain tumor. I hope this is a pay-it-forward book that you can use to guide you and others throughout your life.

I have compiled a fact sheet that may provide you with information that you may not have. I hope this helps, and I know there is no way I can touch on

77

every single situation, so I will tell you as much as I can, especially the information I gathered during my recovery. I must start this by saying: What you think you may know you do not know until after surgery.

- Do not ask other people questions, because everyone is different. *Ask, ask, ask* your doctor.

- Morphine does not work on head pain. I learned this the hard way.

- Never, never have surgery on a Friday. Resident doctors will be taking care of you. You will be miserable all weekend.

- They will tell you that you need another CT scan after surgery, but it should be ultimately up to you.

- I never slept for days after brain surgery, no matter what medicine they gave me. But remember, you could have resident doctors who will not call your usual doctor over the weekend. Make sure you

78

go over your pain management with
your doctor before surgery, and cover
your sleep meds too. Your brain will be
different than before.

- Your spouse is probably not the person
  you want with you after you have brain
  surgery if you are a female. This is based
  on my experience, because even though
  he was protective, a male is not a
  detailed person. Your spouse will be as
  traumatized as you, and you will not be
  able to think straight.

- You will be left alone because family
  has to follow visiting hours. I had no
  visiting after 8:30 PM to 10 AM. For
  me, I was scared to death that I would
  suddenly start bleeding in the brain or
  have a seizure, and that no one would
  know about it.

- Nurses are weekend nurses too. My IV
  was inserted wrong, and it collapsed my
  vein. She changed it right before her
  shift change even though I had brought it

to her attention hours before.

- Using search engines to look things up will only confuse you more, and will not provide accurate information for you.

- Getting multiple MRIs if you are claustrophobic is absolute hell. Ask your doctor ahead of time for a prescription for anxiety meds, and keep your eyes closed during the procedure. Take your favorite CD or MP3 player. For the most part, they will play your own music.

- There is no good tumor. You must live in fear for the rest of your life and will most likely suffer from some type of chronic pain and depression. And most can never work again and will not qualify for any help. But keep trying.

- Do not shave your head or cut your hair short like I did. They used a mustache trimmer and cut an outline for the scar and wet my hair to keep the damage to a minimal.

- Most people will never know you have a brain tumor unless you tell them. Why? Because you look fine or normal to them. It's a hidden disability

- You will suffer fatigue, concentration problems, insomnia, pain, and often chronic pain. I've had pain for eleven years now.

- Your family will not cut you any slack. As stated above, you are healed to them and you will look normal after a few weeks.

- All of the above will cause you mental anguish, depression, and even hard feelings. This will lead to more pain and fatigue. Have a great doctor like your primary care doctor or a neurologist to follow up with. Your neurosurgeon is just for surgery.

- Short-term memory loss may not be a

short-term ailment. This may not happen right after surgery, but as time passes and scar tissue forms, short-term memory loss happens, like it or not. And I am *not* just getting old.

- I once said, "I will never take medicine in my life." Well that went out the window as soon as I was diagnosed. Don't blame the medicine for your issues. I could possibly have some issues from medicine, but how can I live without them?

- You shouldn't drive. *Really?* Yes, at least for six months, and it has been suggested for eleven years now. *How can I not drive? Are you going to take off work and take me places every time I need something?* No. Now don't get me wrong, some will not be able to drive, but most can, however, they are usually limited to familiar places only.

The Day at the Fair

I went to the Texas State Fair
I wanted to be there
With my family at my side
I knew I couldn't cry
So I walked and talked
Hurting but never balked

I love to see my little girl smile
She is the apple of my trial
I wanted her to have everything
But I knew that it wouldn't bring
All the happiness in this world
Is not the money I did twirl

We rode the train to the Fair
I love to see her breathe the air
She was pushed in and all around
I love to hear her little sounds
The animals she petted are so tame
And the horse show was the same

My little girl is growing tall
Before my eyes there's no more small
I used to wrap her in my arms

Oh how she has the charm
I love to see her at the Fair
My dreams my prayers are in his care

To the fair we all went
And a lot of dollars I did spent.
With love, Mimi.

Giving Up Your Career

As my son drove me to my radiation appointment, he asked me, "Mom, why do you think and talk like you are putting me out?" Because it seems as though everyone has to juggle their schedule just for me. It started the day the doctor said I had a brain tumor. When you are diagnosed, the world spins at a whole new level. Plans that you had before are not the plans anymore. New plans are made, and they all revolve around doctors' appointments, CT scans, and MRIs. I wish, oh how I wish I could go back to the day before I found out and just live one more moment of being well, or at least be able to think I was well. I suppose we all long to go back in time for some reason. But this is so life altering. "I am putting you out son." I said. "You could be home with your daughter enjoying your summer."

One of the hardest things I had to do was to give up. But I finally threw in the towel. As hard as I worked to get back on my feet after brain surgery, it had only lasted about three years and I struggled each and every day. My job as a glorified secretary was demanding. The phone, the typing, computer work, and the parents. I worked for the school district, and I know many people believe we don't have that many duties, but we do. We have state and federal mandates as well as local and societal responsibilities to uphold. So the paperwork can be insurmountable at times.

I was lucky in a way, more than most, because my husband worked mostly in the same district. I, like many brain patients, was told not to drive. How can you live life without driving? I know. I know. I became at risk of hurting someone else, so I complied as much as possible. But day after day, my head pain worsened. There were days when I had to stop, turn off the lights, and my head went down. Everyone seemed to support me even though I was not 100%. I worked at about 50%. And the more I tried to work, the harder it became for me. Finally, I decided to resign at the end of the school year, not just from my job, but also from my old life. This was the end of my twenty-three-year career. At first life was like a summer breeze, almost a relief. But soon the depression set in. I was no longer a viable worker who could generate income. From now on my pocket money was going to be running on empty. Additionally, working for a school district in Texas disqualifies you for Social Security.

And somehow, this feeling paralleled the same feeling of how I felt after brain surgery. The world continued to rotate and everyone went on about their way, to work. And I was once again left behind. I had to find my "new normal" all over again. It is very hard to reinvent yourself at fifty years old. *So what do I want to do? What can I do? Oh wait. I don't have any money. Ok, well looks like a garage sale would be my new entertainment...that is when I can catch a ride.* Do you realize that most people in this world work? My family, my friends, my everyone, they all work! Ugh. I am more unemployed, damaged, and a doctor's dream. I am no longer a secretary.

That's Life

Up in the morning things to do
Hurry hurry the house is a zoo
Eat, dress, all the things in a bag
Out the door, time is fast and I lag.
Can't be late, when will this end?
I wish, I wish I could just send
All to work and those to school
Before you know it, all is cool.

Time is measured seconds, minutes, hours
I barely have time to take my shower
Cars, trucks, planes, and trains
Look out the window, it's a shame
God's plan to worship and sing
This world is an opposite sting.
I can't tell if I'm coming or going
All is wrong, my life it's towing.

That's life, it comes and it goes
That's life, starts and finishes

That's life, so long but short
Where did the time go?

Babies come so tiny cute, cuddly too
It is time, off we go, what to do?
We laugh, we cry, we squeeze them tight
We listen to them breathe through the night.
How did they grow up so fast?
It seems we have had a blast.
They are grown, we've let them go
To blossom, to be the best of show.

Tears flow the news is hard
My child it is time for me to go.
I've given you the things you need.
I know, I know, you will succeed.
You've paid me back in leaps and bounds.
I was so proud to hear her pound
Her heart will forever be with me now
To heaven I'm going, we all know how
Stay my little one, I am so proud!

That's Life.

Hidden Disability

From the moment I was diagnosed with a brain tumor until now, I have seen myself as disabled. The problem was, and is, that I didn't know it. For sure, after the brain surgery I couldn't see that I had trouble working. You could definitely see that I was disabled. I had a huge scar in the back of my head and I wore a black patch over my right eye. People stared, and I could only imagine what they were thinking. But as time passed, the scar healed and my patch turned into a normal pair of glasses. Really, you could not even tell I have had brain surgery.

Now I see other people in a whole new light. *Maybe they are disabled, and I wonder what their disability is? They are parking in the disabled parking.* I never really took advantage of the disabled parking spaces over the years, but I became a little disgruntled by the fact that a person would get out of the disabled car but would look normal to me. Was I judging them like I did not want to be judged?

Part of the purpose of this book is to raise

awareness for those who have hidden disabilities. If you apply for disability, you must brave mounds of paperwork and doctors' statements that prove that you have a disability.

As stated, I actually do not qualify for disability, where most people apply to get benefits. Is it fair? I don't really think so, but I can't fight against the government by myself. A disability, by definition, is an impairment, physiological or medical. The person must be unable to perform work, basically. I had a private insurance policy that covered me for five years. Even after I applied, I was appalled that most people do not consider a brain tumor a disability. You know my story. You tell me whether I'm impaired. For this reason, I must speak out and state: don't judge a book by its cover.

I really do look like a very healthy person. Up until about three months ago, I was expected to go from mental work to physical work. Now, I have a tumor on my spine. But when I did apply for my insurance benefit that was the first statement they made. They stated, "You can be retrained to do another type of employment." They denied me several times just like social security would have.

After several tries and an attorney's help, I was finally qualified to receive benefits but with the addition of monthly checks to make sure my situation doesn't change. Ha! Hello! Hello! My brain was damaged. It will never change. I still can't drive and I still have severe head pain. And now my back is broken! Case closed.

For those of you who are still fighting, please do not give up. Brain surgery cripples your brain. You will not be able to do the same schedule as before. There will be changes in your body, mind, and soul forever. But keep going.

For those of you that exist outside of our realm, just because we don't look sick, that doesn't mean that we have been miraculously healed. We do not wear any devices, nor will you know we are disabled.

Brittany Maynard-USA Today

Life, death, love, and separation. Where does it all begin in end? We are put here on earth for a reason. Some get it right, while others do not. Good and evil. While God is all good, there is still evil. Do

91

we get a choice in any of this? And are we supposed to get a choice? We certainly do not get to choose our birth. We start off so very small, with milk as our Manna. We continue to grow; some make it, and some do not. Again, that's not a choice we get to make at an early age.

Cancer has no boundaries. None! Young, old, boy, or girl. So, so sad. Then we crossed the age when we begin to make choices in our own life. What is the magic number? Who knows? God. Not mom or dad, or even you. But it happens. I always pictured it like this: love and good on one side. The other side, the dark side, contains evil or hate and wrongful sin. Thank goodness we have a God that forgives us. His heart is pure, always! He is God, the healer, maker of all, gracious and righteous, and full of compassion. His love endures forever and ever! Psalms 118:29. Life is a blessing. John 6:47. I tell you the truth, he who believes has everlasting life. I have to say I personally, am a Christian. I am a follower of Jesus the Messiah. God formed the man from the dust of the ground and he breathed into his nostrils the breath of life, and man became a living being. Genesis 2:7. In Ecclesiastes 3, God's plan is written by Solomon. There is a time for everything. Never doubt God's timing because you can lose the purpose that God intended for you. Our reward is eternal life. Heaven. What is the purpose of life? Always the purpose is to lift up God, to be in awe, and always revere him until the end of time, whether by death or by life.

Why am I off on this tangent? Because I know so many who have fought the battle of cancer. Also, I have seen the suffering God's people goes through. It doesn't seem fair. But we all have a purpose to fulfill. Is it acceptable to take your own life? No. Our life is a gift, a blessing, and God gave us breath. He gives and he decides when breathe goes. I have lost friends, close friends in their 40s and early 50s. But even when a younger person is in the limelight, we all take notice. It is outside our circle of friends. Brittany Maynard, who had a malignant brain tumor, moved to Oregon from California so she could legally die with medication prescribed by law. So do we get the right to die just because a law says it's legally okay? Her words stated in USA today, "I still feel good enough and I still have enough joy and I still laugh and smile with my family and friends enough that it doesn't seem like the right time right now." This came from a website she

93

started. She went on to say, "But it will come because I feel myself getting sicker. It's happening each week." So I feel her pain and suffering. Even with the stage one meningioma that I had. I have great days, and I have days that put me down and I want to die too. Her symptoms she suffered were seizures, severe headaches, and neck pain, and stroke-like symptoms. If I were to ask a meningioma patient their symptoms, I would guess that at least every person would repeat that they are suffering symptoms just like these. I know her family must have grieved many times as they watch their beloved young woman suffer. If you're reading this, it is likely that you also either know a person that is suffering. That person is chosen to suffer. Why? I have asked myself many times. To repeat some of my story, my mother was taken at twenty-four years old, when I was only two months old. My sister and I, who is three years older than me, were split up. My dad was a basket case while mourning the death of his wife, my mother. He remarried two times, the latter of which was when I was six years old. My sister and I were taken from our grandmother. I was six, young and innocent, and afraid and overshadowed by my new step-mom's two children. I was number one, then I became number four. It turned out that my dad had become very ill with neurofibromatosis. Throughout life events, my dad was absent. He was here in body, but not in a mental state. In other words, I was being a raise by a mean stepmother. Yes, kind of like a Cinderella story. Mom's mom, Granny, promised to get us out of this terrible situation but she died when I was eleven. During all of this time, I was exposed to sexual abuse from the older stepbrother. Yes, this is a secret, one I have had for all of my life until now. It started when I was six and ended when I was about thirteen, when I got old enough to say stop!! You see, there was no real love in my life. No one showed emotions at my house. We were in survival mode, my sister and I. She chose to internalize her tears and mourning. I blocked my hurts all together. At age fifteen, my sister left home, and ran away. My other stepsister did the same thing just to get away from her own mother. I left home when I was sixteen. I could write a whole different book about my life, but I wanted to help others with my words. I was married by age seventeen to a man that I loved dearly. We had two beautiful children, and life was finally like it was supposed to be, kind of.

95

Then one day after my 41st birthday, I woke up with excruciating pain in my head. It was summer time so I was home and everyone else went to work. As the day progressed I started getting sick to my stomach and it became the worst headache anyone could ever imagine. I suffered and till about 2 PM when I called my daughter who worked at the doctor's office. She hurriedly came and got me, and took me through the back door of the office, as I could barely speak or walk.

And the rest is history. A pain shot with anti-nausea medicine and a CT scan.

Of course I did not change after surgery. What is that supposed to mean? I was still the same Kayla going in and coming out. I was so damn determined to jump back on my feet, I kept begging in the doctors for six weeks' release after the brain surgery. Each time I got the same freaking answer, "no!" It takes at least six months for the swelling to go down. Mind you, I still had double vision and only weighed about 100 pounds. And sleep, well, I never slept for days, weeks, months, and now years later, sleep still abates me. But in hindsight, I was so hardheaded. I should've stayed home for the full the six months and recouped. Isn't it funny how you have more answers looking back than you do when you are moving forward? I know that is where prayer and faith come in.

I know so much more now than then. And what's even better is that you know more than me now. We did not have the social media that you have now. I am so glad that you have the opportunity to rely on friends that you've never even met. I don't mention it much, but I do feel like I must add this because a brain tumor changes you and your life so much. The patient does not recognize the subtle changes, but the family does. And what are they supposed to do? *I changed, but my husband didn't?* Maybe the family was trying to help me, but they didn't know how. Maybe, no not maybe, I was a very lonely woman. The brain tumor has put me into a category like no other. I was married to this man for twenty-five years. He was my first love, and he did try many ways to address the "new me." But what once was, was no more. I could not afford to feel lonely. I needed more compassion, which was the opposite of his way of handling me. He said, "Get over it and be glad, you're one of the lucky ones." Oh how many times have we heard this? Once that was said to me, I was done. My emotional side was done. I filed for divorce in the fall of 2004, one year after my surgery.

I want to bring you back to the changes in our lives. No one has control but God Almighty. No one has the answer but God the Father, the Son, and the Holy Spirit. There has not been a day since September 19, 2003, that my head has not hurt, that I have not laughed like I should, that I can enjoy my granddaughter or my children like I used to. My neurosurgeon, my neurologist, my physician's assistant, nor the many other doctors, can ever feel what we feel inside. It is true. Once you open the brain, that person is, well, just a different person. I prayed from the day I found out on June 19, 2003, until the morning of my surgery, for God to please spare my live and let me live again. *Please Lord I am not finished here on earth. I want to see my children be successful. I want to meet their spouses and I want to love my grandchildren. Please, please, please!* And here I am eleven years later, writing this book in order to help others who don't know that they don't know.

How many have gone before me? There have been

98

loved ones, family members, actors, actresses, and many, many, more who have gone before me and have already traveled this journey without any help. They have fought their battles and lost. Just some of the ones that we remember are: Ted Kennedy, Bob O'Connor, Johnny Oates the baseball player, and Fritz Von Eric the wrestler. And as I am writing this book, there are many actors and actresses that are fighting the brain tumor battle. Brain tumors have no boundaries, and they do not discriminate. Most benign tumors do not metastasize into other parts of your body. However, malignant tumors usually metastasize into the parts of your brain or other parts of your body. Did you know that brain tumors are the leading cause of cancer-related death in children? According to the American Brain Tumor Association, in males ages 23-39, they are the second leading cause of death. In females, brain tumors are the fifth leading cause in ages 20 through 39. In a year's time, almost 70,000 new cases of primary brain tumors will be diagnosed. Even worse, our children are being diagnosed between the ages of 0-19. 700,000 people are living with brain tumors, and these are just the diagnosed ones. Many people have them and are not aware of it yet. There are many types of brain tumors and I

99

Association, or the A.B.T.A.

According to the American Cancer Society, the overall chance that a person will develop a malignant brain tumor of the brain or spinal cord is less than 1%. Unfortunately, I fell into the 1%. How lucky is that?

The National Brain Tumor Society states that brain tumors are often deadly, that they impact quality of life, and that they change everything for patients and their loved ones. I have changed, and my family treats me differently too. Why? I believe that they can't handle the thought of their loved one not being the same. I am still human. I still have feelings, and probably get even more hurt and angry than many realize. I believe that many others and I have dramatic brain injury or TBI from the tumor or surgery. When I was diagnosed in 2003, the awareness that we have now, which is still not very much, was not in place, sadly.

My Daily Struggles

Each day is a struggle. From the moment my feet

hit the floor, my body starts to rebel against me. Every joint in my body aches, and my hands and fingers are swollen so much that I can't move them. That's the first symptom that I notice. Then, when I am actually awake, the right side of my head starts to pound. I can feel the quadrant of my brain that was affected the most. There are no words to describe the feeling. My right eye is burning and feels like a stabbing knife in my head.

I have spoken many times to my doctors about the pain, but not one seems to really care anymore. I will have to say that my Pain Management Doctor is the most compassionate, but I do know that the drugs I get from him will most likely be my demise. It's just a matter of time.

I have to make myself stop thinking about all of the above. If I dwell on it, then I get so depressed and it causes so many tears. I just need to survive one day at a time and hope for the future somehow. I am 53, and my parents left this earth early in life. I have to stay positive and get myself going each morning on another task. But the tasks are such obstacles for me. I start out with many tasks for the day and if I can accomplish one or two, then I have done my *do* for the day. I had another word for *do* but I can't remember…there goes my word recall. Gone! It comes and goes. Grr. It is a three ring circus within my body.

I just want to share my feelings with you today. This is not really part of learning about meningiomas but could be detrimental to me. I have had a CT scan, MRIs, blood work, bone scans, x-rays, and genetic testing. They have found an L1 tumor on my spine. I had a bone marrow test and a bone tissue biopsy. I have had one oncologist that said it was benign but I was urged to go for a second opinion by my PM Doctor. I am sitting here waiting for my 3 o'clock appointment, not knowing what the answers are. This is just another pain and another illness that I really do not have time for, and neither does my family. I have to say kudos to my kids though. They call and check on me and offer to go to my appointments. The text me to check on me and offer support. But inside I am crying. No one can see my emotions because I have shoved them far, far, back into my soul. It's just like my meningioma. Life goes on with or without you. So you might as well pick yourself up off the floor, shake it off, and get ready to fight your battle. You

103

are the one who bears all the pain and suffering. Just pray and listen to that inner voice you have become accustomed to. Love and Peace to you all who read this. And for heaven's sake, do not give up. Life is still moving!

So as I am sitting here in the office, I sneak a Xanax and my blood pressure reads 150/84. I know it was higher before I took the medicine but I needed it for my nerves. I am in the little room waiting for the doctor and on time. Remember, I am seeing an oncologist. Do I have cancer? I had a benign brain tumor but now a spinal tumor?

Just leaving the doctor's office now. I have always said, and you can take this to the bank, that you have to be your own of your health care. After having so many tests, you're so scared that your pants fall down. Why can't the health care system have a general computer connection where it is mandatory to put in the results of your tests and reports into one huge server? How much easier would that be? I have waited two weeks to see this doctor and it took almost one hour just to chase down the reports and they still did not have what they needed. Kudos to this doctor and his staff. It is rare to find a doctor that will give 100% to you these days. You look the world over to find true care then you meet another, and *thpttt* they are gone. *Hee Haw…*

Have you ever heard of so many doctors in one's life? Now I'm going to see a Radiation Oncologist. They apparently administer the radiation plan for you. Oh my, I am learning so much and I have already been through the ringer once. I was just told that I might need radiation or surgery and I know I'm still in the battle. I can't really close this chapter yet because I do not know the ending…*A neuriloma? Another tumor?*

Here is another poem I wrote to process my thoughts. I have to find an outlet to express myself. This was written after our daughter in-law and oldest son's baby shower. This will be our sixth grandbaby. God showed me the life process today. We are excited. Babies are born, some die young, and some die old. But we all know the photosynthesis, the life cycle. At 53, I didn't know I would be writing about death again. But then again at 41, my tumor, rang out.

What

It is not good; you are in a bad way.
Those are the words they had to say.
The best we have is what I got
They saved my life I fought
So hard all went well
Who knew I couldn't tell
It hurt like hell
Really never stopped
More pain came down to me.
I just ignored
I couldn't put another thing on my plate
As with 4 kids, 5 grandkids and one on the way

One child has lost her way.
I can't go now I need to stay
My heart is so sad and be it may
The doctor called the test is bad
What? What did you say?
My brain is supposed to be the one who takes
me home
But my back has hurt for years
I have fought back all my tears and fears
I can't complain, it is too cruel
They have endured so much
I can't imagine any more such.
I guess I'll have to wait and see
Just what Jesus has for me.

Pain Management Doctor

I've been to my Pain Management Doctor (or PM) for several years now. After my neurologist gave up on me, he referred me to this type of doctor. I never wanted to ever go to him. I thought a PM doctor was for drug addicts. I was wrong, very wrong. The neurologist couldn't control my pain after trying every pill imaginable. I can't even tell you how heartbroken I was. *A PM doctor? Who are they? What do they do?* The shame I felt was immeasurable. I didn't want anyone to know, and to have to tell my husband was unbearable. But we both agreed to go to this PM doctor. An appointment was made and I waited until that dreaded day. My head was down and there were mounds of paperwork. I had to give my pain on a pain scale about 20 times. "How was your pain last month? On average, how was your pain? Where is your pain? What makes it worse? What makes it better?" Well, by now you get the consensus.

My name was called and I went into a room. The nurse takes your weight, blood pressure, and gets all your current information. In just a few minutes, a little man walked in with a pleasant smile. Not at all what I was expecting. He and his nurse treated me with so much respect. Maybe it was because of the brain tumor, or maybe it was because they were genuine. The PM doctor went over my chart thoroughly and gave me medicines to try. Of course, here we go again. I was lying on my back, hair pinned back, and in came the nurse with the needle injection for the block. About 50 sticks in my forehead later, and we were ready to go. Wow. And why was I ashamed to go to a PM doctor? From that day forward, we tried every nerve block in my neck, and even in my cheeks. We have even tried Botox. But still, the pain was relentless, and I made an appointment in one month to go back.

Did I mention I am not a big fan of doctors? And now I have another one. Let's see, there is my Primary Doctor (I actually love her though), my neurologist, my neurosurgeon, my neurofibromatosis doctor, and my neuropsychologist. Of course there are the extra doctors too, like my dentist, my gastrologist, my gynecologist, and my dermatologist. I could go on, but those were my main ones. Many, many times,

109

the PM doctor had done his magic, for lack of a better phrase. When he tried all the meds, we began doing procedures, which was really his specialty. He was originally an anesthesiologist and went on to pain management. I can honestly say now, that I am very proactive towards pain management. Still, I have had everything done to me that the pigs would eat. And today (4/1/2014), I awoke with a massive head pain. I probably overdid it the day before. I love to be physical, but I certainly pay for it the next day.

So are you in pain? I've learned from all my experiences, 12 years and counting, that there are two types of pain management doctors. One is the type who just writes prescriptions and goes on to the next patient, and the other type will do procedures. That is where the money is at, but he is proactive in getting you off your pain medicines. What do I mean by procedures? In an outpatient setting, doctors inject nerve blocks where the pain is coming from. My procedures are not always spot on, but when they are, I have pain relief for three months. The doctor says he will not do another procedure on me because it would be out of desperation and he will not do that. If the procedure

would work on me every time, then he would
continue that protocol.

So month after month I go in for my two
prescriptions and cry every time because I do not
want green eggs and ham. Or a spoonful of sugar to
help the medicine go down. I want answers. It's
been years and I love my pain management doctor.
He is very compassionate and knows I am a "legit"
patient, not a drug addict.

Let's just take this one step further. We, my
husband and I, are out the door, going to get my
prescription filled. Now remember I was 41 when I
was diagnosed, and had never taken a pill on a
regular basis, and BAM! I have to have one of those
pill keepers for Sunday – Thursday, AM and PM,
and a pill splitter. I'm hoping to get better and get
off every pill. I want off these meds. Okay, no
problem. Wait. Oh. Let me talk to the pharmacist.
So now I feel like a prisoner again and the warden
has his whip, ready to snap. I didn't ask for this
stupid brain tumor. Thank you very much! A little
anger, let loose. The pharmacist says, "Well we can
fill these but we are out and this is a prescription.

111

DUH! Like I don't know that. It doesn't matter where I go, no one wants to fill my prescription. In essence, it makes me look even worse because I have to try different pharmacies most, each time leaving in tears as though I was a bad person for having a brain tumor.

One day, I went to this pharmacy chain store because I could get the prescription filled in Texas or Arkansas. Smart, right? Nope. He, the pharmacist, chewed me out one side and down the other for wanting them to fill my prescription. It was so bad that I had to call my husband from work to take me home. Later, I made one last effort to get my prescription filled. I went in and thought, maybe since this was a small pharmacy I could get some sympathy. I was met by Joe from the other big box pharmacy, the pharmacist who had chewed me out, and I said, oh hell no.

"I know you. You are the pharmacist from the other pharmacy. Excuse me, but I believe I have made a mistake because there is no way in hell that that man would ever get my business."

"Wait, don't go. I need to tell you something. I am not that type of man. The big store limited me from speaking to you about their policies and those drugs

112

were on the list." I glared at him. Was I to trust him? It sounded right. I handed my prescription to him. "I will do everything in my power to help you. Please Mrs. Ross, give me a chance." So I did. Ever since then he has been my go-to-guy for all my prescriptions. Sometimes I have to go to Texas for a week and then I run out. Oh boy! That just kills me, but on Monday I get back on track. What a life after a brain tumor. A "new normal."

Family

As I reflect on all my family members, those who are here and those who have left behind their legacy, I can feel each member's energy, whether it has been positive or negative. When a person gets "sick," people tend to ignore them because they really do not know what to say, or they are afraid that their words might offend you somehow. I have to admit; I am guilty myself of doing the same thing. The looks I got once word got out. A brain tumor? My church, my friends, even complete strangers, they all say I'll pray for you or I am sorry. It just seemed like that at the time, which was June 19th,

113

one day after my 41st birthday. Up until then, I had always been the healthiest of all. I watched my weight, I exercised, and I ate right, almost a complete vegetarian.

So where was my family? My diagnosis hit me like a huge boulder that came from the sky and landed right on my head. Now please don't take this the wrong way because I had beautiful, wonderful friends. But all of my family had obligations such as: 1. Jobs, 2. Their own tug and pull, and 3. Everyone seemed to think that someone else was already stepping up to take me to all of my tests. I saw doctor after doctor. My husband took the brunt of all the trips. Thank you Lord for providing him the days off. His work was kind of a family business that had grown large. They told him to go and not worry about his job at the time. So he was beside me every step of the way. He was really like my best friend. We did everything together. My dear son had just graduated high school. He was a handsome, tall man, and very protective of his mother. My children always came first. He was having some health related issues. I thought it was just a UTI so I sent him to the doctor, and he was there for a very long time. And I couldn't drive after my brain tumor diagnosis, so he drove himself. After his dad was home from work I sent him up to the doctor's office to check on him. He was diagnosed with Type 2 diabetes which turned out to be Type 1 after we almost lost him at college. He was in his dorm and a friend tried to wake him and he couldn't wake up so she called the ambulance. That day was just unbearable for me as a mother. After much insulin, the Lord gave him back his life that day, but not before he saw a glimpse of heaven where a loved one came to him. All of this at the same time was a lot for him and me.

My daughter, who is the oldest child, worked at the clinic that diagnosed me. She was actually the one I called that one day when I woke up with head pain, nausea, and that was the worst day ever. She came to get me and took me in the back door to the P.A. who insisted I have the CT scan that saved my life. As I said, God was in control, but when you go through something severe like a brain tumor, everything is a big, big blur. I was and I am blessed to have two beautiful children who care.

Now my family has grown to two children: one daughter in law, and a granddaughter. I also have two stepchildren, and five grandchildren from them. All are dear to my heart and each one of them mean love to me. It's been twelve years and in another story in another chapter, I will explain the hurt and loneliness of having an illness. Until then, just know I am blessed and sing the song, "O What a Day That Will Be When My Jesus I Shall See, O What A Day That will be.

Stay Busy

You need to stay busy. Find something to occupy your brain. My brain functions only when it gets a notion. Not always when I need it to either. *What all have I tried?* Remember, your neurotransmitters don't fire together any more. They are scrambled from the trauma resection. I worked as long as I possibly could, even to the point where I would take my pillow and crawl under my desk. I would try to hide away the pain and because my husband was the boss, but we both knew I had reached my limits. During this time, I applied for my private disability insurance policy. The days were long, and I pretended, but there were days where my brain was sharper. You learn how to pretend to be normal, to hide the pain and hope it just goes away. I had medicine all of the time but it was not strong enough to get the pain under control. I went into a downward spiral at my last job. And yes, stress was a big part, and it seemed to never go away. It was the end of my career. So now my husband goes to work and leaves me at home every day. We ended up moving jobs to another state and of course, I did not know anyone. I had to change again to another "new normal." We left our four children and grandchildren, which left me with a broken heart, but with God we can prevail. We started traveling to Texas a lot. I am a hard worker, not afraid to get dirty, but when I tried to mow the lawn, or anything equal to that, I would be in bed for the entirety of the next day. But I needed to do something. After all, I was only 49, and I had lots of time left to inspire my artistic side. A typical day was to get up with my husband, my head killing me, but I kept the schedule because I did not want to let down my dear husband. I would send him off to work, well dressed, fed, and with a kiss goodbye. I cleaned, picked up, and laid down until almost eleven o'clock when I pushed myself to get up and start lunch. Lunch was the biggest meal of the day and he came home every day to eat. Lunch was cooked,

117

but not the way I used to cook, but nonetheless food was on the table. Then I would get him back out the door and to bed I went again. I cried so, so much. I knew I was dying. But if you know me, I am not the type of person who gives up. I needed to find something to keep me busy. I knew our income had dropped drastically when I stopped working. I felt I must do something to help out. At the time, couponing was a big deal. I bought papers, clipped coupons, found groups on Facebook, and got every coupon matched to the sales ad. I was going to get some good free deals, or I thought I was going to anyway. I put so much work into couponing, and even tried to teach others what I was doing so they could save money as well. I have to say, I was about 20% successful. That did not work. Failure.

Then I thought I would recruit my husband and get him to help me. But he was not into it and he could not care less if I got a roll of deodorant for $0.15 or not. First of all, the big stores drive me crazy, the noise, the loud speakers, and people are everywhere. But I would try and I would send my husband for a box of cereal, and he would come back with a giant box of something he liked, ignoring the brand or size. I honestly believed it cost more money than saving. And I was left with a big nervous meltdown. I went back to bed, covers over my head. Each day I would look forward to my husband going to work going back to bed and I had my schedule down to a science. I knew if I went back to bed at 1 PM I could sleep until 3:30, and it would be time for my husband to come back home. I went into survival mode with my thoughts. I did not like to be by myself or without my husband.

I went on to the next project. I used to sew a lot and I thought I would sew for my granddaughters. As a matter of fact, I sewed almost all of my daughter's clothes when she was a baby and when she was a little girl. And I would even sew my husband's western shirts, snaps, yokes, and trim. I loved to sew. I went to a sewing store that I found on the Internet. Boy, was this guy a good salesman. I bought the featured electronic, digital brand new sewing machine. And for a bonus he threw in an embroidery machine too. Sounds like a Lucy and Ethel story, right? What a deal! I bought every accessory imaginable. I had not sewed in years, pre-brain tumor. Every color thread, cutting boards, spool holders, and I even talked my husband into

119

buying a table great for sewing. After all, I was going to sew for those granddaughters. I bought patterns, material, and scissors. Well by now you are getting the picture. I read all I could for the day and never looked at it again. That digital sewing machine was so far above my new ability to use. I just kept making excuses why I hadn't sewed. I tried a couple more times on that machine and all I go out of it was a big headache. I couldn't imagine touching the embroidery machine. It was never opened. Well, here come the tears. I never knew I had so many tears! Failure! Coupons, then the sewing machine which had cost $1000.00 and let's not forget the extra $400 for the throw-in embroidery machine.

Failure, failure, and more failure. Do you ever wonder why I look so depressed? Well, back to bed, my drawing board. I wanted to sleep, sleep, sleep but I never can. I have too much energy. And I need to find something else to do. This has been almost a year now.

Through all of this, I'll leave out all the details like how we've moved again. Maybe, just maybe, it was the house that depressed me so much. And the new house is bigger, that way we have more room to sew. My hubby, said, "Throw away those damn coupons, we don't need them." So we went from a one-bedroom house to a three-bedroom house. One bedroom was ours, and one was for company, which we hardly ever had. But we do have four kids and maybe they will come. Anyway, one bedroom is now my stuff/sewing room.

But one day, I came across this store. I love garage sales, and they had garage sale/estate sale furniture. The furniture they had was being painted and distressed. I called up the one friend I had met, our landlord. She is a beautiful gal with the heart of Texas even though she and I were living in Arkansas.

This new place had classes at night, but I never drive at night, and I pretty much don't drive at all. I talked her into taking me. We were supposed to take a piece of furniture to class and we were going to learn how to distress and potentially sell our items. Oh boy, this was right up my alley. That night, with furniture tucked in the back of my friend's SUV, we took the class and we both made the prettiest furniture ever. I was so proud, excited, and did I

121

mention tired? I usually hit the hay around 7 PM and it was almost 9 PM, but, my friend and I hit every estate sale, every garage sale, and we bought the paint, brushes, furniture, and everything else we needed. This was when the chalk paint craze was going on and it was very expensive to buy. But I needed something to do. We had so much stuff we started storing our finds in her husband's back room at work. I worked eagerly. This didn't require a lot of reading. The only problem was that we had bought so much stuff and had no place to market all of our newly painted pieces. You can never guess what comes next. We visited an antique store, and I love antiques, and always have. We even went to auctions, and we were on a roll. But that antique store was particularly enticing because they had booths, so I called up my hubby and asked, "What would you think if my friend and I rented a booth?" He never tells me no; he just makes it happen for me. And guess what? The antique store just happened to have a small booth open and she said if I came immediately I could have it. So I rented the booth! It was fun, and the little booth became too small, so we asked for a bigger booth. We moved into it with the help of my friend's husband who thinks we are both crazy. But hey, we were like two peas in a pod. Days passed and we sold some, but then months passed and we sold little. Well you get it by now, we couldn't get the booth any fuller and we were paying rent. In essence, we were going in the hole every month. We closed the booth down. Like always, I did forget to mention that we also started making burlap wreaths. I think I may have sold one out of the fifteen or so I had made. The rest went into storage. The bigger house with three bedrooms was full of junk. *What now?* I had a big, big mess. I couldn't market this stuff from my house so I had a big garage sale by myself and with my bestie. We made a few pennies and sold a lot of our junk, and we collected for pennies on the dollar. Here come the tears.

By this time, I needed therapy. But I kept pushing myself on, and even at Christmas I made every type of candy there was. My grandmother had passed this tradition down to me and I wanted to teach my children. Everything I tried I burned that year. Oops. I couldn't begin to tell you how sad that was. I would look at the recipe (which I had never needed before) and I couldn't get from step one to step two without reading it four or five times. All of my previous knowledge left me when the tumor did. I really did get therapy after all of this. A neuropsychologist, she was wonderful in telling me how to change my way of thinking. She said that I had been way too hard on myself. Well, I am 50 years old and my family still sees me as mom. I am a failure! Tumor, tumor, tumor! Sigh.

What's next? Well by everyone else's standards, I am about done. I just need to relax, watch TV, and don't get so upset. They say "I would love to stay home and do nothing." Ha! I still work my butt off doing house chores. Let's just say I have tried EBay, Amazon, Facebook, and anything else to stay busy. And each time Failure follows me. Tumor! You get the idea by now. I know I am not a failure, but I still have not found that niche of things I can do effortlessly.

This information is for the caregiver. The caregiver is a lifesaver for the brain tumor patient, and can be helpful in the recovery process if they understand what is going on in the patient's brain. Please learn to give the patient more time, and please have patience. Remember, this person has to reinvent who they are at their core. They will experience fatigue, memory issues, difficulty in concentration, and overall dysfunction. They will need extra time to complete a task and this may not go away with time. This may be their "new normal," but they have to go through several processes to find their "new normal." For myself, buying a big bill of groceries was impossible, and I started using a small list. I was the person who paid the bills every other week, but I started making mistakes and paying bills out of the wrong accounts, so my husband had to take this responsibility from me. If the patient gets in a crowd of people, they may withdraw and ask to leave. The chaos of large groups may disorientate the patient and cause them to avoid crowds. I have been blamed for behavior-type problems, but really, I am having issues with coping. All of these things, and everyday life issues become struggles, and the caretaker must play a vital role in the patient's life recovery. Please never be condescending to me, or talk to me like a child. My brain is injured, just like how you may have a broken leg and need crutches. We need time and coaching, not constructive criticism. I am not just being sensitive to you. My emotions and of ability to function normally are not what they used to be. So please learn to be patient, and help me with encouragement, instead of telling me I need

125

My Sister

My sister and I were once so close
Everyone could only visit for a dose
Of love and laughter many we shared.
Every day seemed like she cared.
Many days have passed now, months and years,
And my sister and I share no more tears.
Time has passed, words are said,
But my sister's love, my tears were shed.
Who is this person who stole her from me?
I ask, I ask? Who could it be?
We shared so much from the start,
Only we know what's in the heart.
My dear I see you from above,
I have left you with my love.
As I write the tears does flow,
Please get back to where you show
All those around left to survive
And look no more for those who cry.
Cause all have gone before us,
They always knew it was a must.
I love you dear sister now,
But day, months, years, too late now.

The Real Me

I would rarely express myself this way, but please know that it *is* important for me to tell my story. My life is one big medical mishap. I have already told you what happened and how I am, but my day-to-day trials reveal so much more that I have not put on paper. Every day is a question. *Will I wake up and be able to function?* At age 53, most people would chock up my forgetfulness to age. I know, however, that my inadequacies are not age related. I find it aggravating that there are studies on MTBI or Mild Traumatic Brain Injury that always refer to war or car accidents. MTBI can also be derived from having brain surgery. We get a bad rap because we did not have a big accident or fight a war. We actually have fought a war. Our own war is going on in our heads as the tumor invades places it shouldn't. And the excavation of that darn thing is more than traumatic, so where is our study? All we have is each other.

Today I am listening to my mind and it is evaluating whether or not I can socialize today. It is a Monday, and I have survived another weekend. Yes, I said *survived.* I must adjust my mind and my way of thinking, from cleaning up from the weekend to thinking about cooking for the week, or for the day. It is a little over a week until Thanksgiving, and I still do not have a definitive answer on who is coming. Now most people would just adjust their cooking portions, but not a brain tumor patient. It is a big deal. I want so badly to be normal and do a quick clean of my house, run off to the grocery store, no list in hand because I would remember everything. I have memories of my grandmother's meals embedded in my brain. Problem is: a) I'm not my grandmother b) in everyone's eyes she was perfect c) I can't even peel the potatoes and cook the turkey at the same time. In other words, the multitasking tool in my brain is gone. According to *Recovering from Mild Traumatic Brain Injury* by Mary Ann Keatley, PhD. and Laura L. Whitmore, much of the brain's energy is used to filter out unnecessary information. This is telling me that after brain injury, a person loses their brain filter. And according to them, the brain is mostly used for functioning and the filter is the last thing it does. They go on to say that going into a restaurant or store where there are fluorescent lights, background music, and a lot of stimuli, may cause the brain to shut down. This is not an excuse for bowing out

129

gracefully from going out or not visiting family in an environment that is not conducive for quiet, less active happenings. I have been accused, talked about behind my back, and even called names like "selfish" by people I love. I wish they could read just a smidgen of what I have read. I read to understand myself so I can understand how I feel. I feel guilty, and sometimes my family makes me feel guilty for having these deficits. Don't they know that if I could go back and chose to not have this happen, I would? And what scares the hell out of me is the memory part of my brain. Where is it going? It is definitely going somewhere, but I don't want to end up in a nursing home at age 60. I have tried to tell my children that I have these issues and I know they can see them too, but do they really want to process this as this is happening to their mother? And my husband, I tell him I am struggling, and he just says, "Kayla, I know." We all just hope it doesn't get any worse. When will they say to me, "Mom, you are not functioning in a way that you need too"? It is like dementia or Alzheimer's disease? I am looking forward to yet another Thanksgiving, but I wonder if this is going to be my last Thanksgiving, or whether I will remember my grandchildren's names. I am not balloon waiting to pop. That is the first thing you feel in the morning. So I turn to medication to help relieve the pain. Taking medication is not the road that I ever thought I would go down. I believed at age 40 that I would never take any medicine or ever consider using marijuana to control the pain. I remember how my dad, who had the same disease I have, would come home every day for a pain shot injection. He had a drawer in the kitchen that housed his pain pills. I was a little girl then, and didn't understand the scope of what my dad had suffered. I wish I could go back and tell him I understand and I support him. Support and acknowledgement mean everything to a brain tumor patient. We do not get that from our doctors. It's pretty cut and dry from their standpoint. My desire to go shopping is non-existent, and that is not normal. However, the battle of the mind begins when you walk out of the safety of your own home. For years, I had panic attacks when I would get in the car to run to town. My heart pounded, my eyes became full of water that rolled down my cheeks. I had medicine for anxiety, but that was just a minimal…something. I have lost my word again. That happens all the time. When I do go shopping, I am a bit cheap and I like to use my coupons. But where did I put them? And now I am spending more money than I wanted too. There are lots of people, lights, music, and then there is remembering where you parked. Oh my! Where did I park? I prefer to stay at home and stay in the protection of the four walls that house me. Am I normal? NO! I know because at 40, before my brain tumor, I could run a marathon on a shopping day and I wanted to go by myself. That way I could focus on everything I wanted or needed. I miss those days. I juggled my work, my family, being a wife, and taking care of my 88-year-old grandmother. I went to sporting events with my children and volunteered at different levels, depending on where they needed me. When I look back at my life, especially after the diagnosis, I know that those things have been ripped away from me because of this darn tumor. Oh how I want my life back!

Whirlwind

My head is in a whirlwind today
All I want is my head to stay
For I cannot show you how
My head and heart should feel now.
I try to put them into words to say
I've got to rest now must delay
I love to work get up and play
But my head is in a whirlwind today.

Wash and dry the clothes a must
I have to I promise to trust
All I have for you my love
Your heart is brought like a dove
Things that separate us apart
All my love is in our hearts.

Get up, Get up, go your way
My head is in a whirlwind today
I have so much to say and do.
Most of you has no clue
How it feels to express my hurts.
I've got to go now to get his shirts.

My head is in a whirlwind today.
I am so scared, I am afraid.
My whirlwind head is here to stay.

My Back Tumor

I have another tumor
In this there is no humor.
My tumor was gone for long
And I thought of it like a song,
With verses and an end
With words but no bends.

How did this happen to me?
This is something I couldn't foresee.
A tumor not in my head but back
Of all the knowledge I did lack.
Now no surgery is possible but how?

No words, no action just a tumor
Oh how I wish it was just a rumor
My back, my back, how could this be?
It hurts, It hurts, as you will see
This tumor is no rumor.

As I have been writing, all of the information has
been about my brain tumor. But as my life unfolds,
and since I am an advocate for get better medical
care, especially for those with hidden disabilities, I

136

must write this chapter for those that suffer a more silent disease, Neurofibromatosis.

As a little girl, I watched my Dad suffer tumor after tumor. He had over twenty surgeries all over his body ranging from his back to his legs, his neck, and nearly all of his extremities. One of his surgeries crippled him because they had to cut the tumor out of his nerve. He endured so much pain. I observed his daily routine of taking pain pills, getting pain shots at home, and having to come home and rest to make it through a day's work. Of course, as a youngster, my formed opinion, remembering I had no mother, was that whatever he was occupied with stole him away from me. I couldn't understand his pain and suffering then, but as I look back I owe him a huge apology. Since he is no longer alive there is no way to say, "Hey Dad, I understand your suffering." I also suffer now. I know he would have been my support person because he had gone through everything I am going through.

I had a brain tumor, yes, but now I have a new tumor. It first started about 2 years ago. I had pain in my right hip. It was not a sciatic pain, but felt more like a broken hip. It hurt to lie down and sit for long periods of time. I endured this for as long as I could. The burning, gnawing pain persisted and finally I spoke to my pain management doctor. He gave me injections, but to no avail, for the pain was still there. That day he ordered an MRI, and from there was like 0-90 in one day.

He also knew this oncologist, he said that he was very good and came from UT Southwestern in Dallas. That was where I had my brain surgery. This would be my second opinion and remember, everyone needs a second opinion. I was very glad I took his advice. He probably saved me from being paralyzed the rest of my life.

I first turned to a neurosurgeon to get this spindle cell neoplasm tumor out of my L1 on my spine. He said that he could not do surgery. This was because it was in a very precarious place and way too close to my nerves. The words he used were *paralyzed, screws, rods,* and *extreme pain.* He said he would not do it. I was left hanging for a couple of weeks. Don't you hate the wait? I do! But when I finally got in to see the oncologist, I discovered that he was the most thorough doctor. Now I was impressed. He got the ball rolling by requesting all my records, biopsies, and bloodwork. The oncologist set me up to see yet another neurosurgeon. Like I needed another doctor, right? But realization sets in, and now I am on track for several new appointments. I am seeing a radiation oncologist too. Does this mean I need radiation? Well yes, that is exactly what I learned when I went to see this doctor. That was a Monday, and I was scheduled for a Wednesday setup. This is all new to me. I never had radiation with my brain tumor. What does the setup mean? A CT scan with tattoos all over my abdomen and back. With brain surgery, it was in on Friday, and out on Tuesday. He wanted to start this process as soon as possible, but the doctor has to set up the machine and computer just for you so the radiation will spot-radiate with ions in the desired area. Whew!

So I am set for a Monday start, and I was told that I could drive myself, but I have had many family and friends to offer to drive me. Keeping in mind the fact that my brain tumor still rules over me and my head every day of my life, I accepted their offer.
"Mrs. Ross?"
"Yes," I answered.

"Hello, I will be your radiation therapist for the next six weeks. Here is your gown, please come out when you get ready."

Do I want to come out? No. Do I have to do this? Yes.

"Come and lie down face up and don't move."

It was like a portable CT scan that moved around you. It had a big screen, and a big x-ray type machine that surrounded you. I held onto a bar above my head, and no movement was allowed. That was when the therapist came in with the needles that were going to tattoo me for the rest of my life.

"This is where the beams of radiation are going to enter your body." She said.

Three injections, three stings, and yes, I now have tattoos that I never intended to have. But once again, life threw me a curve ball and now I am tattooed! All is done for the first day, and only 29 more to go.

Days come and go, and I make it through with a lot of help and of course it is not without many incidents, such as new plans, and my brain often goes crazy every few days because of the barometric pressure. I know those who are brain patients can relate to the head insanity when the weather changes or when fronts come through. And even though I am fighting a new tumor, my head is still the same. I journal my way through each day and will enlighten you with information as it comes to light. I do not want to leave out anything that might help someone else in this situation. But, at the same time, I do not want to bore you with the details of a tumor outside of the brain tumor subject.

Remember to take a nice warm blanket with you each time. I have finished my radiation, and the radiation oncologist thinks it is time to go see another neurosurgeon for yet another opinion. I wonder if I am being passed off because the radiation is not working. I have so many questions, but no answers. It is no different than when I had my brain tumor. I will be writing about the neurosurgeon's diagnosis. This will be my second opinion. Ironically, the doctors work at the same office but have different opinions.

As this new journey unfolds, so do the questions, doctor visits, tests, and bloodwork all over again. I wonder if I am ready for yet another "new normal" in my life. I wonder if I can jump to the next lily pad. Even though I am a veteran of the health care

141

system, so much has changed since I had my craniotomy. I have gone to four different doctors now, and three have told me to wait and watch. So I will. And then, I will have a whole new story to tell. Wait and Watch.

I will be your God through all your lifetime…
I made you and I will care for you.
I will carry you along and be your Savior.

ISIAH 4 6:4 TLB

CPSIA information can be obtained
at www.ICGtesting.com
Printed in the USA
LVOW03s1431070317
526425LV00014B/1730/P